Federal Benefits for Veterans, Dependents, and Survivors

Federal Benefits for Veterans, Dependents, and Survivors

Updated Edition

The US Department of Veterans Affairs

810 Vermont Ave., N.W.
Washington, DC 20420

Skyhorse Publishing

Visit our website at www.skyhorsepublishing.com.

10 9 8 7 6 5 4 3 2 1

Library of Congress Cataloging-in-Publication Data is available on file.

Print ISBN: 978-1-62914-579-2
Ebook ISBN: 978-1-62914-946-2

Cover design by Richard Rossiter

Printed in the United States of America

Contents

Introduction

Veterans of the United States armed forces may be eligible for a broad range of benefits and services provided by the U.S. Department of Veterans Affairs (VA). Some of these benefits may be utilized while on active duty. These benefits are codified in Title 38 of the United States Code. This booklet contains a summary of these benefits effective Jan. 1, 2013. For additional information, visit www.va.gov/.

La versión en español de este folleto se encuentra disponible en formato Adobe Acrobat a través de el link: http://www.va.gov/opa/publications/benefits_book/federal_benefits_spanish.pdf

General Eligibility: Eligibility for most VA benefits is based upon discharge from active military service under other than dishonorable conditions. Active service means full-time service, other than active duty for training, as a member of the Army, Navy, Air Force, Marine Corps, Coast Guard, or as a commissioned officer of the Public Health Service, Environmental Science Services Administration or National Oceanic and Atmospheric Administration, or its predecessor, the Coast and Geodetic Survey.

Dishonorable and bad conduct discharges issued by general courts-martial may bar VA benefits. Veterans in prison must contact VA to determine eligibility. VA benefits will not be provided to any Veteran or dependent wanted for an outstanding felony warrant.

Certain VA Benefits Require Wartime Service: under the law, VA recognizes these periods of war:

Mexican Border Period: May 9, 1916, through April 5, 1917, for Veterans who served in Mexico, on its borders or in adjacent waters.

World War I: April 6, 1917, through Nov. 11, 1918; for Veterans who served in Russia, April 6, 1917, through April 1, 1920; extended through July 1, 1921, for Veterans who had at least one day of service between April 6, 1917, and Nov. 11, 1918.

World War II: Dec. 7, 1941, through Dec. 31, 1946.

Korean War: June 27, 1950, through Jan. 31, 1955.

Vietnam War: Aug. 5, 1964 (Feb. 28, 1961, for Veterans who served "in country" before Aug. 5, 1964), through May 7, 1975.

Gulf War: Aug. 2, 1990, through a date to be set.

Important Documents

In order to expedite benefits delivery, Veterans seeking a VA benefit for the first time must submit a copy of their service discharge form (DD-214, DD-215, or for World War II Veterans, a WD form), which documents service dates and type of discharge, or provides full name, military service number, and branch and dates of service.

The Veteran's service discharge form should be kept in a safe location accessible to the Veteran and next of kin or designated representative.

The following documents will be needed for claims processing related to a Veteran's death:

1. Veteran's marriage certificate for claims of a surviving spouse or children.
2. Veteran's death certificate if the Veteran did not die in a VA health care facility.
3. Children's birth certificates or adoption papers to determine children's benefits.
4. Veteran's birth certificate to determine parents' benefits.

eBenefits

eBenefits is a joint VA/Department of Defense (DoD) Web portal that provides resources and self-service capabilities to Servicemembers, Veterans, and their families to apply, research, access, and manage their VA and military benefits and personal information through a secure Internet connection.

Through eBenefits Veterans can: apply for benefits, view their disability compensation claim status, access official military personnel documents (e.g., DD Form 214, Certificate of Release or Discharge from Active Duty), transfer entitlement of Post-9/11 GI Bill to eligible dependents (Servicemembers only), obtain a VA-guaranteed home loan Certificate of Eligibility, and register for and update direct deposit information for certain benefits. New features are added regularly.

Accessing eBenefits: The portal is located at www.ebenefits. va.gov. Servicemembers or Veterans must register for an eBenefits account at one of two levels: Basic or Premium. A Premium account allows the user to access personal data in VA and DoD systems, as well as apply for benefits online, check the status of claims, update address records, and more. The Basic account allows access to information entered into eBenefits by the Servicemember or Veteran only. Basic accounts cannot access VA or DoD systems.

Servicemembers can obtain immediate Premium level access by following step-by-step instructions using their Common Access Card (CAC).

In order to register for an eBenefits account, Veterans must be listed in the Defense Enrollment Eligibility Reporting System (DEERS) and first obtain a DoD Self Service (DS) Logon. Note: For those without a DEERS record, VA will first need to verify military service and add the information to DEERS. This is most likely for Veterans who served prior to 1982. Individuals should contact a VA regional office for assistance in being added to DEERS.

A DS Logon is an identity (user name and password) that is used by various DoD and VA Websites, including eBenefits. Those registered in DEERS are eligible for a DS Logon. A DS Logon is valid for the rest of your life.

Identity verification: Many people will be able to verify their identity online by answering a few security questions. A few may need to visit a VA regional office or TRICARE Service Center to have their identities verified. Servicemembers may verify their identity online by using their Common Access Card.

Military retirees may verify their identity online using their Defense Finance and Accounting Service (DFAS) Logon. Veterans in receipt of VA benefits via direct deposit may have their identity verified by calling 1-800-827-1000 and selecting option 7. eBenefits users with Premium access with appropriate My HealtheVet access can login to their My HealtheVet account using the single sign on feature.

Abbreviations

ALS – Amyotrophic Lateral Sclerosis
CHAMPVA – Civilian Health and Medical Program of VA
CLC – Community Living Center
C&P – Compensation and Pension
COE – Certificate of Eligibility
CRDP – Concurrent Retirement and Disability Payments
CRSC – Combat-Related Special Compensation
CWT – Compensated Work Therapy
CZTE – Combat Zone Tax Exclusion
DIC – Dependency and Indemnity Compensation
DoD -- Department of Defense
FHA – Federal Housing Administration
FSGLI – Family Servicemembers' Group Life Insurance
HUD – Department of Housing and Urban Development
IRR – Individual Ready Reserve
MGIB – Montgomery GI Bill
MIA – Missing in Action
NPRC – National Personnel Records Center
NSLI – National Service Life Insurance
OEF – Operation Enduring Freedom
OIF – Operation Iraqi Freedom
OND – Operation New Dawn
OPM – Office of Personnel Management
POW -- Prisoner of War
PTSD – Post-Traumatic Stress Disorder
SAH – Specially Adapted Housing
SBA – Small Business Administration
S-DVI – Service-Disabled Veterans' Insurance
SGLI – Servicemembers' Group Life Insurance
SSB – Special Separation Benefits
TAP – Transition Assistance Program
TSGLI – Servicemembers' Group Life Insurance Traumatic Injury Protection
USCIS – U.S. Citizenship and Immigration Services
USDA – U.S. Department of Agriculture
VA – Department of Veterans Affairs
VEAP – Veterans Educational Assistance Program
VEOA – Veterans' Employment Opportunities Act
VGLI – Veterans' Group Life Insurance
VHA – Veterans Health Administration
VMET – Verification of Military Experience and Training
VMLI – Veterans' Mortgage Life Insurance
VR&E – Vocational Rehabilitation and Employment
VSI – Voluntary Separation Incentive
WAAC – Women's Army Auxiliary Corps
WASPs – Women Air Force Service Pilots

Chapter 1

Health Care Benefits

VA operates the nation's largest integrated health care system with more than 1,500 sites of care, including hospitals, community clinics, community living centers, domiciliaries, readjustment counseling centers, and various other facilities. For additional information on VA health care, visit: www.va.gov/health.

Basic Eligibility

A person who served in the active military, naval, or air service and who was discharged or released under conditions other than dishonorable may qualify for VA health care benefits. Reservists and National Guard members may also qualify for VA health care benefits if they were called to active duty (other than for training only) by a Federal order and completed the full period for which they were called or ordered to active duty.

Minimum Duty Requirements: Veterans who enlisted after Sept. 7, 1980, or who entered active duty after Oct. 16, 1981, must have served 24 continuous months or the full period for which they were called to active duty in order to be eligible. This minimum duty requirement may not apply to Veterans discharged for hardship, early out or a disability incurred or aggravated in the line of duty.

Enrollment

For most Veterans, entry into the VA health care system begins by applying for enrollment. Veterans can now apply and submit their application for enrollment (VA Form 1010EZ), online at www.1010ez.med.va.gov/sec/vha/1010ez/. If assistance is needed while completing the on-line enrollment form, an online chat representative is available to answer questions Monday - Friday between 8 a.m. and 8 pm EST. Veterans can also enroll by calling 1-877-222-VETS (8387) Monday through Friday, 8 a.m. to 8 p.m. Eastern time, or at any VA health care facility or VA regional benefits office. Once enrolled, Veterans can receive health care at VA health care facilities anywhere in the country.

Veterans enrolled in the VA health care system are afforded privacy rights under federal law. VA's Notice of Privacy Practices, which describes how VA may use and disclose Veterans' medical information, is also available on line at www.va.gov/vhapublications/viewpublication.asp?pub_ID=1089

The following four categories of Veterans are not required to enroll, but are urged to do so to permit better planning of health resources:

1. Veterans with a service-connected disability of 50 percent or more.
2. Veterans seeking care for a disability the military determined was incurred or aggravated in the line of duty, but which VA has not yet rated, within 12 months of discharge.
3. Veterans seeking care for a service-connected disability only.
4. Veterans seeking registry examinations (Ionizing Radiation, Agent Orange, Gulf War/Operation Iraqi Freedom/Operation New Dawn and Depleted Uranium).

Priority Groups

During enrollment, each Veteran is assigned to a priority group. VA uses priority groups to balance demand for VA health care enrollment with resources. Changes in available resources may reduce the number of priority groups VA can enroll. If this occurs, VA will publicize the changes and notify affected enrollees. A description of priority groups follows:

Group 1: Veterans with service-connected disabilities rated 50 percent or more and/or Veterans determined by VA to be unemployable due to service-connected conditions.

Group 2: Veterans with service-connected disabilities rated 30 or 40 percent.

Group 3:
Veterans who are former POWs.
Veterans awarded the Purple Heart Medal.
Veterans awarded the Medal of Honor.
Veterans whose discharge was for a disability incurred or aggravated in the line of duty.
Veterans with VA service-connected disabilities rated 10 percent or
20 percent.
Veterans awarded special eligibility classification under Title 38, U.S.C., § 1151, "benefits for individuals disabled by treatment or vocational rehabilitation."

Group 4:
Veterans receiving increased compensation or pension based on their need for regular aid and attendance or by reason of being permanently housebound.
Veterans determined by VA to be catastrophically disabled.

Group 5:
Nonservice-connected Veterans and noncompensable service-connected Veterans rated 0 percent, whose annual income and/or net worth are not greater than the VA financial thresholds.
Veterans receiving VA Pension benefits.
Veterans eligible for Medicaid benefits.

Group 6:
Compensable 0 percent Service-connected Veterans.
Veterans exposed to ionizing radiation during atmospheric testing or during the occupation of Hiroshima and Nagasaki.
Project 112/SHAD participants.
Veterans who served in the Republic of Vietnam between Jan. 9, 1962 and May 7, 1975.
Veterans who served in the Southwest Asia theater of operations from Aug. 2, 1990, through Nov. 11, 1998.
Veterans who served in a theater of combat operations after Nov.11, 1998, as follows:
Veterans discharged from active duty on or after Jan. 28, 2003, for five years post discharge;
Veterans who served on active duty at Camp Lejeune for not fewer than 30 days beginning Jan. 1, 1957 and ending Dec. 31, 1987.

Group 7:
Veterans with incomes below the geographic means test income thresholds and who agree to pay the applicable copayment.

Group 8:
Veterans with gross household incomes above the VA national income threshold and the geographically-adjusted income threshold for their resident location and who agrees to pay copayments. Veterans eligible for enrollment: Noncompensable 0-percent service-connected and:

Subpriority a: Enrolled as of Jan. 16, 2003, and who have remained enrolled since that date and/ or placed in this subpriority due to changed eligibility status.

Subpriority b: Enrolled on or after June 15, 2009 whose income exceeds the current VA National Income Thresholds or VA National Geographic Income Thresholds by 10 percent or less

Veterans eligible for enrollment: Nonservice-connected and
    Subpriority c: Enrolled as of Jan. 16, 2003, and who remained enrolled since that date and/ or placed in this subpriority due to changed eligibility status

Subpriority d: Enrolled on or after June 15, 2009 whose income exceeds the current VA National Income Thresholds or VA National Geographic Income Thresholds by 10 percent or less

Veterans NOT eligible for enrollment: Veterans not meeting the criteria above:
    Subpriority e: Noncompensable 0 percent service-connected
    Subpriority f: Nonservice-connected

VA's current income thresholds can be located at: http://www.va.gov/ healthbenefits/cost/income_thresholds.asp

Recently Discharged Combat Veterans

Veterans, including activated reservists and members of the National Guard, are eligible for the enhanced Combat Veteran benefits if they served on active duty in a theater of combat operations after Nov. 11, 1998, and have been discharged under other than dishonorable conditions.

Effective Jan. 28, 2008, combat Veterans discharged from active duty on or after Jan. 28, 2003, are eligible for enhanced enrollment placement into Priority Group 6 (unless eligible for higher enrollment Priority Group placement) for five-years post discharge.

Veterans receive VA care and medication at no cost for any condition that may be related to their combat service.

Veterans who enroll with VA under this Combat Veteran authority will remain enrolled even after their five-year post discharge period ends. At the end of their post discharge period, VA will reassess the Veteran's information (including all applicable eligibility factors) and make a new enrollment decision. For additional information, call 1-877-222-VETS (8387), Monday through Friday between 8:00 a.m. and 8:00 p.m. Eastern time.

Special Access to Care

Service-Disabled Veterans: who are 50 percent or more disabled from service-connected conditions, unemployable due to service-connected conditions, or receiving care for a service-connected disability receive priority in scheduling of hospital or outpatient medical appointments.

Women Veterans

Women Veterans are eligible for the same VA benefits as male Veterans. Comprehensive health services are available to women Veterans including primary care, specialty care, mental health care, residential treatment and reproductive health care services

VA provides management of acute and chronic illnesses, preventive care, contraceptive and gynecology services, menopause management, and cancer screenings, including pap smears and mammograms. Maternity care is covered in the Medical Benefits package. Women Veterans can receive maternity care from an OB/GYN, family practitioner, or certified nurse midwife who provides pregnancy care.

VA covers the costs of care for newborn children of women Veterans for seven days after birth. Infertility evaluation and limited treatments are also available. Women Veterans Program Managers are available at all VA facilities to assist women Veterans in their health care and benefits. For more information, visit http://www.womenshealth. va.gov/.

Military Sexual Trauma

Military sexual trauma (MST) is the term that the Department of Veterans Affairs uses to refer to sexual assault or repeated, threatening sexual harassment that occurred while the Veteran was serving on active duty (or active duty for training if the service was in the National Guard or Reserves). VA health care professionals provide counseling and treatment to help Veterans overcome health issues related to MST. Veterans who are not otherwise eligible for VA health care may still receive these services. Appropriate services are provided for any injury, illness or psychological condition related to such trauma. For additional information visit: http://www.mentalhealth. va.gov/msthome.asp

Veterans with Spinal Cord Injury/Disorders

There are 24 VA medical centers in the United States with specialized centers (called Spinal Cord Injury Centers) for Veterans with spinal cord injuries and disorders (SCI/D). Comprehensive rehabilitation, SCI/D specialty care, medical, surgical, primary, preventive, psychological, respite, and home care are provided at these centers by interdisciplinary teams which include physicians, nurses, therapists (physical, occupational, kinesiotherapists, therapeutic recreation), psychologists, social workers, vocational counselors, dieticians, respiratory therapy, and other specialists as needed.

There are five Spinal Cord Injury (SCI) Centers that provide long term care for Veterans with SCI/D. In VA facilities that do not have SCI Centers, there is a designated team that consists of a physician, nurse, and social worker to address primary care needs for Veterans with SCI/D and to make referrals to SCI Centers. These SCI Centers and the teams in facilities that do not have centers, comprise the VA SCI System of Care. Some of the services provided in this system of care include rehabilitation, prosthetics and durable medical equipment, orthotics, sensory aids, assistive technology, environmental modifications, telehealth, ventilator weaning and care, chronic pain management, mental health treatment, drivers training, peer counseling, substance abuse treatment, vocational counseling, and caregiver training and support.

There is a long-standing Memorandum of Agreement between VA and the Department of Defense (DoD) to provide specialized care at VA medical facilities for Active Duty Servicemembers who have sustained a spinal cord injury. Ongoing collaboration and education between VA and DoD ensures continuity of care and services. For more information about SCI/D care and the eligibility requirements for the above benefits and services, contact your local VA SCI/D Center and/or visit http://www.sci.va.gov.

OEF/OIF/OND Care Management

Each VA medical center has an OEF/OIF/OND Care Management team in place to coordinate patient care activities and ensure that

Servicemembers and Veterans are receiving patient-centered, integrated care and benefits. OEF/OIF/OND clinical case managers screen all returning combat Veterans for the need for case management services to identify Veterans who may be at risk so VA can intervene early and provide assistance. Severely ill or injured Servicemembers/Veterans are provided with a case manager and other OEF/OIF/OND Servicemembers/Veterans are assigned a case manager as indicated by a positive screening assessment or upon request. OEF/OIF/OND case managers are experts at identifying and accessing resources within their health care system as well as in the local community to help Veterans recover from their injuries and readjust to civilian life.

Financial Assessment

Most Veterans not receiving VA disability compensation or pension payments must provide a financial assessment to determine whether they are below VA income thresholds. VA is currently not enrolling new applicants who decline to provide financial information unless they have a special eligibility factor exempting them from disclosure. VA's income thresholds are located at: www.va.gov/healtheligibility/Library/AnnualThresholds.asp

The financial assessment includes all household income and net worth, including Social Security, retirement pay, unemployment insurance, interest and dividends, workers' compensation, black lung benefits and any other income. Also considered are assets such as the market value of property that is not the primary residence, stocks, bonds, notes, individual retirement accounts, bank deposits, savings accounts and cash.

Medical Services and Medication Copayments

Some Veterans are required to make copayments (copays) to receive VA health care and/or medications.

Inpatient Care: Priority Group 7 and certain other Veterans are responsible for paying 20 percent of VA's inpatient copay or $236.80 for the first 90 days of inpatient hospital care during any 365-day period. For each additional 90 days, the charge is $118.40. In addition, there is a $2 per diem charge.

Priority Group 8 and certain other Veterans are responsible for VA's inpatient copay of $1,184 for the first 90 days of care during any 365-day period. For each additional 90 days, the charge is $592. In addition, there is a $10 per diem charge.

Extended Care: Veterans may be subject to a copay for extended care services. The copay is determined by a calculation using information from completion of VA Form 10-10EC, Application for Extended Care Services.

VA social workers or case managers will counsel Veterans or their family representatives on their eligibility and copay requirements. The copay amount is based on the Veteran's financial situation determined upon application for extended care services and can range from $0 to a maximum copayment amount of $97 a day.

NOTE: Veterans determined to be catastrophically disabled are exempt from copays applicable to the receipt of noninstitutional respite care, noninstitutional geriatric evaluation, noninstitutional adult day health care, homemaker/home health aide, purchase skilled home care, home-based primary care, hospice services and any other noninstitutional alternative extended care services.

Outpatient Care: While many Veterans qualify for free healthcare services based on a VA compensable service-connected condition or other qualifying factor, most Veterans are asked to complete an annual financial assessment, to determine if they qualify for free services. Veterans whose income exceeds the established VA Income Thresholds as well as those who choose not to complete the financial assessment must agree to pay required copays to become eligible for VA healthcare services.

> Primary Care Services: $15
> Specialty Care Services: $50

NOTE: Copay amount is limited to a single charge per visit regardless of the number of health care providers seen in a single day. The copay amount is based on the highest level of service received.

Outpatient Visits Not Requiring Copays: Certain services are not charged a copay. Copays do not apply to publicly announced VA health fairs or outpatient visits solely for preventive screening and/ or vaccinations, such as vaccinations for influenza and pneumococcal, or screening for hypertension, hepatitis B, tobacco, alcohol, hyperlipidemia, breast cancer, cervical cancer, Human papillomavirus (HPV), colorectal cancer by fecal occult blood testing, education about the risks and benefits of prostate cancer screening, HIV testing and prevention counseling (including the distribution of condoms), and weight reduction or smoking cessation counseling (individual and group). Laboratory, plaim film radiology, electrocardiograms, and hospice care and in-home video telehealth are also exempt from copays. While hepatitis C screening and HIV testing and counseling are exempt, medical care for HIV and hepatitis C are NOT exempt from copays.

Medication: While many Veterans are exempt for medication co-pays, nonservice-connected Veterans in Priority Groups 7 and 8 are charged $9 for each 30-day or less supply of medication provided on an outpatient basis for the treatment of a nonservice-connected condition. Veterans enrolled in Priority Groups 2 through 6 are charged $8 for each 30-day or less supply of medication; the maximum copay for medications that will be charged in calendar year 2013 is $960 for nonservice-connected medications.

NOTE: Copays apply to prescription and over-the-counter medications, such as aspirin, cough syrup or vitamins, dispensed by a VA pharmacy. Copays are not charged for medical supplies, such as syringes or alcohol wipes. Copays do not apply to condoms.

Health Savings Accounts (HSA) can be utilized to make VA copayments. HSAs are usually linked to High Deductible Health Plans (HDHPs).

Private Health Insurance Billing

VA is required to bill private health insurance providers for medical care, supplies and medications provided for treatment of Veterans' non-service connected conditions. Generally, VA cannot bill Medicare, but can bill Medicare supplemental health insurance for covered services. VA is authorized to bill and accept reimbursement from High Deductible Health Plans (HDHPs) for care provided for non-service connected conditions.VA may also accept reimbursement from Health Reimbursement Arrangements (HRAs) for care provided for non-service connected conditions.

All Veterans applying for VA medical care are required to provide

information on their health insurance coverage, including coverage provided under policies of their spouses. Veterans are not responsible for paying any remaining balance of VA's insurance claim not paid or covered by their health insurance, and any payment received by VA may be used to offset "dollar for dollar" a Veteran's VA copayment responsibility.
J9

All Veterans applying for VA medical care are required to provide information on their health insurance coverage, including coverage provided under policies of their spouses. Veterans are not responsible for paying any remaining balance of VA's insurance claim not paid or covered by their health insurance, and any payment received by VA may be used to offset "dollar for dollar" a Veteran's VA copay responsibility.

Release of Information (ROI) for Sensitive Diagnosis

An ROI authorization form VAF 10-5345 is a VA standard form used to obtain authorization to release sensitive (protected) health information to an insurance company for purposes of reimbursement.. Veterans/patients who were treated or offered treatment for a sensitive condition of drug abuse, alcohol abuse or alcoholism, HIV testing or treatment, and Sickle Cell Anemia or Trait must provide written authorization to allow VA to release their sensitive information to a third party (insurance company).

NOTE: Please note that if the ROI authorization form is not completed and signed, the VA cannot bill the insurance company for non-service connected care. Thus if the Veteran is required to pay a copayment for health visits, the Veteran will be responsible for the entire copayment amount as VA will not be able to credit account dollar for dollar based on what the insurance company has reimbursed.

Reimbursement of Travel Costs

Eligible Veterans may be provided mileage reimbursement or, when medically indicated, special mode transport (e.g. wheelchair van, ambulance) when traveling for approved VA medical care.

Mileage reimbursement is 41.5 cents per mile and is subject to a deductible of $3 for each one-way trip and $6 for a round trip; with a maximum deductible of $18 or the amount after six one-way trips (whichever occurs first) per calendar month.

The deductible may be waived when travel is in relation to a VA compensation or pension examination; travel is by special mode; or when imposition would cause a severe financial hardship.

Eligibility: The following are eligible for VA travel reimbursement:
Veterans rated 30 percent or more service-connected .
Veterans traveling for treatment of service-connected conditions.
Veterans who receive a VA pension.
Veterans traveling for scheduled compensation or pension examinations.
Veterans whose income does not exceed the maximum annual VA pension rate.
Veterans in certain emergency situations.
Veterans whose medical condition requires a special mode of transportation and travel is pre-authorized. (Advanced authorization is not required in an emergency and a delay would be hazardous to life or health).
Certain non-Veterans when related to care of a Veteran (Caregivers, attendants & donors).

Beneficiary travel fraud can take money out of the pockets of deserving Veterans. Inappropriate uses of beneficiary travel benefits include: incorrect addresses provided resulting in increased mileage; driving/riding together and making separate claims; and taking no cost transportation, such as DAV, and making claims. Veterans making false statements for beneficiary travel reimbursement may be prosecuted under applicable laws.

Reporting Fraud: Help VA's Secretary ensure integrity by reporting suspected fraud, waste or abuse in VA programs or operations.

VA Inspector General Hotline
P.O. Box 50410
Washington, DC 20091-0410
E-mail: vaoighotline@va.gov
VAOIG hotline 1-800-488-8244
Fax: (202) 565-7936

VA Medical Programs

Veteran Health Registries
Certain Veterans can participate in a VA health registry and receive
free evaluations. These evaluations include a medical history, physical exam, and if deemed necessary by the clinician, laboratory tests
or other studies. VA maintains health registries to provide special
health evaluations and health-related information. To participate,
contact the Environmental Health Coordinator at the nearest VA
health care facility or visit www.publichealth.va.gov/exposures to see
a directory which lists Environmental Health Coordinators by state
and U.S. territory.
Veterans should be aware that a health registry evaluation is not a
disability compensation exam. A registry evaluation does not start a
claim for compensation and is not required for any VA benefits.

Gulf War Registry: For Veterans who served on active military
duty in Southwest Asia during the Gulf War, which began in 1990
and continues to the present, and includes Operation Iraqi Freedom (OIF) and Operation New Dawn (OND). The Gulf War registry
was designed to identify possible health effects resulting from U.S.
military personnel service in certain areas of Southwest Asia. Potential exposures include endemic infectious diseases and hazardous
occupational or environmental exposures, including heavy metals,
air pollutants (particulate matter and gases such as nitrogen oxides,
carbon monoxide sulfur oxides, hydrocarbons).

Depleted Uranium Registries: Depleted uranium (DU) is uranium left over after most of the more radioactive U-235 isotope has
been removed. DU possesses about 60 percent of the radioactivity
of naturally occurring uranium; it is a radiation hazard only in very
large exposures for prolonged time. DU has some chemical toxicity
related to being a heavy metal (similar to lead) which occurs at lower
doses and is the main concern for Veterans with embedded DU frag-
ments.

Veterans who are identified by the Department of Defense (DoD)
or have concerns about possible depleted uranium exposure are
eligible for a DU evaluation at their local facility.

Agent Orange Registry: Agent Orange is an herbicide the U.S.
military used between 1962 and 1971 during the Vietnam War to remove jungle that provided enemy cover. Veterans serving in Vietnam

were possibly exposed to Agent Orange or its dioxin contaminant. Veterans eligible for this registry evaluation are those who served on the ground in Vietnam between Jan. 9,1962, and May 7,1975, regardless of the length of service; this includes Veterans who served aboard boats that operated on inland waterways ("Brown Water Navy") or who made brief visits ashore.

 Other Veterans with possible exposure who are eligible include those who served: along the demilitarized zone in Korea (between April 1, 1968 and Aug. 31, 1971), on certain bases or in certain units in Thailand (between Feb. 28, 1961 and May 7, 1975), or on certain U.S. bases or locations in other countries where Agent Orange or other herbicides were tested or stored.

VA maintains a DoD-provided list of locations and dates where Agent Orange or other herbicides were tested or stored at military bases in the U.S. or locations in other countries at www.publichealth.va.gov/exposures. For sites not listed, the Veteran should provide some proof of exposure to obtain a registry examination. Information is also available through VA's Special Issues Helpline at 1-800-749-8387.

Ionizing Radiation Registry: For Veterans in receipt of nasopharyngeal (nose and throat) radium irradiation treatments while in the active military, naval, or air service and Veterans possibly exposed to, and who are concerned about, possible adverse effects of their atomic exposure during the following "radiation-risk activities" –

On-site participation in:
        an atmospheric detonation of a nuclear device, whether or not the testing nation was the United States;
        occupation of Hiroshima or Nagasaki from Aug. 6, 1945, through July 1, 1946; or
        internment as a POW in Japan during World War II, which the Secretary of Veterans Affairs determines resulted in an opportunity for exposure to ionizing radiation comparable to that of Veterans involved in the occupation of Hiroshima or Nagasaki, or

Service at (VA regulations provide that "radiation-risk activity" refers to):
        Department of Energy gaseous diffusion plants at Paducah, Kentucky, Portsmouth, Ohio, or the K-25 area at Oak Ridge, Tennessee, for at least 250 days before Feb. 1, 1992, if the Veteran was moni-

tored for each of the 250 days using dosimetry badges to monitor radiation to external body parts; or

Amchitka Island, Alaska, before Jan. 1, 1974, if the Veteran served for at least 250 days in a position that had exposures comparable to a job that was monitored using dosimetry badges in proximity to Longshot, Milrow, or Cannikin underground nuclear tests.

Readjustment Counseling Services

VA provides outreach and readjustment counseling services through 300 community-based Vet Centers located in all 50 states, the District of Columbia, Guam, Puerto Rico, and America Samoa.

Eligibility: Veterans are eligible if they served on active duty in a combat theater or area of hostility during World War II, the Korean War, the Vietnam War, the Gulf War, or the campaigns in Lebanon, Grenada, Panama, Somalia, Bosnia, Kosovo, Afghanistan, Iraq and the Global War on Terror. Veterans, who served in the active military during the Vietnam-era, but not in the Republic of Vietnam, must have requested services at a Vet Center before Jan. 1, 2004. Vet Centers do not require enrollment in the VHA Health Care System.

Services Offered: Vet Center counselors provide individual, group, and family readjustment counseling to combat Veterans to assist them in making a successful transition from military to civilian life; to include treatment for post-traumatic stress disorder (PTSD) and help with any other military related problems that affect functioning within the family, work, school or other areas of everyday life. Other psycho-social services include outreach, education, medical referral, homeless Veteran services, employment, VA benefit referral, and the brokering of non-VA services. The Vet Centers also provide military sexual trauma counseling to Veterans of both genders and of any era of military service.

Bereavement Counseling related to Servicemembers: Bereavement counseling is available through VA's Vet Centers to all immediate family members (including spouses, children, parents, and siblings) of Servicemembers who die while serving on active service. This includes federally-activated members of the National Guard and reserve components. Vet Center bereavement services for surviving family members of Servicemembers may be accessed by calling (202) 461-6530.Vet Center Combat Call Center (1-877-WAR-VETS) is an around the clock confidential call center where combat Veterans and their families can call to talk about their military experience or any other issue they are facing in their readjustment to civilian life. The staff is comprised of combat Veterans from several eras as well as family members of combat Veterans. For additional information, contact the nearest Vet Center, listed in the back of this book, or visit www.vetcenter.va.gov/.

Vet Center Combat Call Center: (1-877-WAR-VETS) is an around the clock confidential call center where combat Veterans and their families can call to talk about their military experience or any other issue they are facing in their readjustment to civilian life. The staff is comprised of combat Veterans from several eras as well as family members of combat Veterans.

Prosthetic and Sensory Aids

Veterans receiving VA care for any condition may receive VA prosthetic appliances, equipment and services, such as home respiratory therapy, artificial limbs, orthopedic braces and therapeutic shoes, wheelchairs, powered mobility, crutches, canes, walkers, special aids, appliances, optical and electronic devices for visual impairment and other durable medical equipment and supplies. Veterans who are approved for a guide or service dog may also receive service dog benefits including veterinary care and equipment.

VA medical services include diagnostic audiology and diagnostic and preventive eye care services. VA will provide hearing aids and eyeglasses to the following Veterans:

(a) Those with any compensable service-connected disability.
(b) Those who are former Prisoners of War (POWs).
(c) Those who were awarded a Purple Heart.
(d) Those in receipt of benefits under Title 38 United States Code (U.S.C.) 1151.
(e) Those in receipt of an increased pension based on being rated permanently housebound or in need of regular aid and attendance.
(f) Those with vision or hearing impairment resulting from diseases or the existence of another medical condition for which the Veteran is receiving care or services from VHA, or which resulted from treatment of that medical condition, e.g., stroke, polytrauma, traumatic brain injury, diabetes, multiple sclerosis, vascular disease, geriatric chronic illnesses, toxicity from drugs, ocular photosensitivity

from drugs, cataract surgery, and/or other surgeries performed on the eye, ear, or brain resulting in vision or hearing impairment.

(g) Those with significant functional or cognitive impairment evidenced by deficiencies in the ability to perform activities of daily living. but not including normally occurring visual or hearing impairments. Note: Veterans with normally occurring visual and/or hearing impairments that interfere with their medical care are eligible for eyeglasses and hearing aids.

(h) Those who have vision or hearing impairment or combined visual and hearing impairments severe enough that it interferes with their ability to participate actively in their own medical treatment. **Note:** The term "severe" is to be interpreted as a vision and/or hearing loss that interferes with or restricts access to, involvement in, or active participation in health care services (e.g., communication or reading medication labels). The term is not to be interpreted to mean that a severe hearing or vision loss must exist to be eligible for hearing aids or eyeglasses.

(i) Those Veterans who have service-connected which contribute to a loss of communication ability; however, hearing aids are to be provided only as needed for the service-connected hearing disability.

Nonservice-connected (NSC) Veterans are eligible for hearing aids or eyeglasses on the basis of medical need. All such Veterans (including Medal of Honor recipients who do not have entitling conditions or circumstances and catastrophically disabled Veterans) must receive a hearing evaluation by a state-licensed audiologist prior to determining eligibility for hearing aids or an appropriate evaluation by an optometrist or ophthalmologist prior to determining eligibility for eyeglasses to establish medical justification for provision of these devices. These Veterans must meet the following criteria for eligibility based on medical need:

(a) Be enrolled at the VA medical facility where they receive their health care; and

(b) Have hearing or vision loss that interferes with or restricts communication to the extent that it affects their active participation in the provision of health care services as determined by an audiologist or an eye care practitioner or provider.

For additional information, contact the prosthetic chief or representative at the nearest VA medical center or go to www.prosthetics.va.gov.

Home Improvements and Structural Alterations

VA provides up to $6,800 lifetime benefits for service-connected
Veterans/Servicemembers and up to $2,000 lifetime benefit for or
nonservice-connected Veterans to make home improvements and/or
structural changes necessary for the continuation of treatment or for
disability access to the Veterans/Servicemembers home and essential lavatory and sanitary facilities.

Modifications can include but are not limited to:
   Ramps allowing entrance to, or exit from, the Veterans/Service-
members primary residence; Widening of doorways to allow access to essential lavatory and sanitary facilities; Raising or lowering
kitchen or bathroom sinks and/or counters; Improving entrance paths
or driveways in immediate area of the home to facilitate access to
the home by the Veteran/Servicemember; Improving plumbing or
electrical systems made necessary due to installation of dialysis
equipment or other medically sustaining equipment in the home.
For application information, contact the Prosthetic Representative at
the nearest VA medical center.

Special Eligibility Programs

Special Eligibility for Children with Spina Bifida: VA provides
comprehensive health care benefits, including outpatient, inpatient,
pharmacy, prosthetics, medical equipment, and supplies for certain
Korea and Vietnam Veterans' birth children diagnosed with Spina
Bifida (except spina bifida occulta).
**Special Eligibility for Veterans Participating in Vocational Re-
habilitation:** Veterans participating in VA's vocational rehabilitation
program may receive VA health care benefits including prosthetics,
medical equipment, and supplies.

Limitations on Benefits Available to Veterans outside the U.S.:
Veterans outside the U.S. are eligible for prosthetics, medical equipment, and supplies only for a service-connected disability.

Services for Blind and Visually Impaired Veterans

Severely disabled blind Veterans may be eligible for case management services at a VA medical center and for admission to an
inpatient or outpatient VA blind or vision rehabilitation program. In
addition, blind Veterans enrolled in the VA health care system may
receive:

1. A total health and benefits review as well as counseling on obtaining benefits that may be due to the Veteran but have not been received.
2. Adjustment to blindness training and counseling.
3. Home improvements and structural alterations.
4. Specially adapted housing and adaptations.
5. Automobile grant.
6. Rehabilitation assessment and training to improve independence and quality of life.
7. Low-vision devices and training in their use.
8. Electronic and mechanical aids for the blind, including adaptive computers and computer-assisted devices such as reading machines and electronic travel aids.
9. Facilitation and recommendation for guide dogs and support in the use of guide dogs.
10. Costs for veterinary care and equipment for guide dogs.
11. Talking books, tapes and Braille literature.
12. Family education and support.

Eligible visually impaired Veterans (who are not severely visually disabled) enrolled in the VA health care system may be eligible for services at a VA medical center or for admission to an outpatient VA blind rehabilitation program and may also receive:

1. A total health and benefits review.
2. Adjustment to vision loss counseling.
3. Rehabilitation assessment and training to improve independence and quality of life.
4. Low-vision devices and training in their use.
5. Electronic and mechanical aids for the visually impaired, including adaptive computers and computer-assisted devices, such as reading machines and electronic travel aids, and training in their use.
6. Family education and support.

Mental Health Care Treatment

Veterans eligible for VA medical care may receive general and specialty mental health treatment as needed. Mental health services are available in primary care clinics (including Home Based Primary Care), general and specialty mental health outpatient clinics, inpatient mental health units, residential rehabilitation and treatment programs, specialty medical clinics, and Community Living Centers. Mental Health services are also available in medical settings in which patients are receiving treatment, such as inpatient medicine and out-patient specialty medical clinics. In addition to general mental health care, this may include specialized PTSD services, treatment for Veterans with psychological conditions related to a history of military sexual trauma, psychosocial rehabilitation and recovery services, treatment for substance use disorders, suicide prevention programs, geriatric mental health problems, violence prevention, evidence-based psychotherapy programs, treatment with psychiatric medications consistent with VA Clinical Practice Guidelines , integrated care services, and mental health disaster response/post deployment activities.

Specialized programs, such as mental health intensive case management, psychosocial rehabilitation and recovery centers, and work programs are provided for Veterans with serious mental health problems. VA's Program of Comprehensive Assistance for Family Caregivers entitles the designated primary and secondary Family Caregiver(s) access to mental health. These services may be offered at the VA and/or contracted agencies. General Caregivers (of all era Veterans) can receive counseling and other services when necessary if the treatment supports the Veteran's treatment plan. For more information on VA Mental Health services visit http://www.mentalhealth.va.gov/VAMentalHealthGroup.asp

Veterans Crisis Line: Veterans experiencing an emotional distress/crisis or who need to talk to a trained mental health professional may call the Veterans Crisis Line 1-800-273-TALK (8255). The hotline is available 24 hours a day, seven days a week. When callers press "1", they are immediately connected with a qualified and caring provider who can help.

Chat feature: Veterans Chat is located at the Veterans Crisis Line and enables Veterans, their families and friends to go online where they can anonymously chat with a trained VA counselor. Veterans Chat can be accessed through the suicide prevention Website www.Veterancrisisline.net by clicking on the Veterans Chat tab on the right side of the Webpage.

Text feature: Those in crisis may text 83-8255 free of charge to receive confidential, personal and immediate support.

European access: Veterans and members of the military community in Europe may now receive free, confidential support from the European Military Crisis Line, a new initiative recently launched by VA. Callers in Europe may dial 0800-1273-8255 or DSN 118 to receive confidential support from responders at the Veterans Crisis Line in the U.S. For more information about VA's suicide prevention program, visit: http://www.mentalhealth.va.gov/suicide_prevention/ or www.veteranscrisisline.net.

Make the Connection Resources: help Veterans and their family members connect with information and services to improve their lives. Visitors to MakeTheConnection.net will find a one-stop resource where Veterans and their family and friends can privately explore information, watch stories similar to their own, research content on mental health issues and treatment, and easily access support and information that will help them live more fulfilling lives.

At the heart of Make the Connection are powerful personal testimonials, which illustrate true stories of Veterans who faced life events, experiences, physical injuries or psychological symptoms; reached out for support; and found ways to overcome their challenges. Veterans and their families are encouraged to "make the connection" - with strength and resilience of Veterans like themselves, with other people who care, and with information and available resources for getting their lives on a better track. For more information, go to www.MakeTheConnection.net

Coaching Into Care: works with family members or friends who become aware of the Veteran's post-deployment difficulties, and supports their efFt.s to find help for the Veteran. This national clinical service provides information and help to Veterans and the loved ones who are concerned about them. More information about the service can be found at http://www.mirecc.va.gov/coaching/contact.asp

VA's National Center for PTSD serves as a resource for healthcare professionals, Veterans and families. Information, self-help resources, and other helpful information can be found at www.ptsd.va.gov.

The PTSD Coach is a mobile application that provides information about PTSD, self assessment and symptom management tools and provides information about to connect with resources that are available for those who might be dealing with post trauma effects. The PTSD Coach is available as a free download for iPhone or Android devices.

Mental Health Residential Rehabilitation

Mental Health Residential Rehabilitation Treatment Programs (MH RRTP) (including domiciliaries) provide residential rehabilitative and clinical care to Veterans who have a wide range of problems, illnesses, or rehabilitative care needs which can be medical, psychiatric, substance use, homelessness, vocational, educational, or social. The MH RRTP provides a 24-hour therapeutic setting utilizing a peer and professional support environment. The programs provide a strong emphasis on psychosocial rehabilitation and recovery services that instill personal responsibility to achieve optimal levels of independence upon discharge to independent or supportive community living. MH RRTP also provides rehabilitative care for homeless Veterans.

Eligibility: VA may provide domiciliary care to Veterans whose annual gross household income does not exceed the maximum annual rate of VA pension or to Veterans the Secretary of Veterans Affairs determines have no adequate means of support. The copays for extended care services apply to domiciliary care. Call the nearest benefits or health care facility to obtain the latest information.

Outpatient Dental Treatment

Dental benefits are provided by VA according to law. In some instances, VA is authorized to provide extensive dental care, while in other cases treatment may be limited by law. This Fact Sheet table describes dental eligibility criteria and contains information to assist Veterans in understanding their eligibility for VA dental care.

By law, the eligibility for Outpatient Dental Care is not the same as for most other VA medical benefits. It is categorized in classes. Those eligible for VA dental care under Class I, IIC, or IV are eligible for any necessary dental care to maintain or restore oral health and masticatory function, including repeat care. Other classes have time and/or service limitations.

*Note: Public Law 83 enacted June 16, 1955, amended Veterans' eligibility for outpatient dental services. As a result, any Veteran who received a dental award letter from VBA dated before 1955 in which VBA determined the dental conditions to be noncompensable are no longer eligible for Class II outpatient dental treatment.

Veterans receiving hospital, nursing home, or domiciliary care will be provided dental services that are professionally determined by a VA

If you:	You are eligible for:	Through
Have a service-connected compensable dental disability or condition.	Any needed dental care.	Class I
Are a former prisoner of war.	Any needed dental care.	Class IIC
Have service-connected disabilities rated 100 percent disabling, or are unemployable and paid at the 100 percent rate due to service-connected conditions.	Any needed dental care. [note: Veterans paid at the 100 percent rate based on a temporary rating, are not eligible for comprehensive outpatient dental services.	Class IV
Apply for dental care within 180 days of discharge or release from of active duty (under conditions other than dishonorable) of 90 days or more during the Gulf War era.	One-time dental care if a DD214 certificate of discharge does not indicate that a complete dental examination and all appropriate dental treatment had been rendered prior to discharge.(NOTE)	Class II
Have a service-connected noncompensable dental condition or disability resulting from combat wounds or service trauma.	Any dental care necessary to provide and maintain a functioning dentition. A Dental Trauma Rating (VA Form 10-564-D) or VA Regional Office Rating Decision letter (VA Form 10-7131) identifies the tooth/teeth that are trauma rated.	Class IIA
Have a dental condition clinically determined by VA to be associated with and aggravating a service-connected medical condition.	Dental care to treat the oral conditions that are determined by a VA dental professional to have a direct and material detrimental effect to a service-connected medical condition.	Class III
Are actively engaged in a 38 USC Chapter 31 vocational rehabilitation program.	Dental care to the extent necessary to: to enter, achieve goals, and prevent interruption of a rehab program; hasten the return to a rehab program because of a dental condition; or to secure and adjust to employment during employment assistance, or enable to achieve maximum independence in daily living.	Class V
Are receiving VA care or are scheduled for inpatient care and require dental care for a condition complicating a current medical condition	Dental care to treat the oral conditions that are determined by a VA dental professional to complicate a medical condition currently under treatment.	Class VI
Are an enrolled Veteran who may be homeless and receiving care under VHA Directive 2007-039.	A one-time course of dental care that is determined medically necessary to relieve pain, assist in gaining employment, or treat moderate to severe gingival and periodontal conditions.	Class IIB

dentist, in consultation with the referring physician, to be essential to the management of the patient's medical condition under active treatment. For more information about eligibility for VA medical and dental benefits, contact VA at 1-877-222-8387 8387, Monday through Friday between 8:00am and 8:00pm Eastern time or www.va.gov/healthbenefits

Vocational and Work Assistance Programs

VHA provides vocational assistance and therapeutic work opportunities through three primary **Therapeutic & Supported Employment Services (TSES) programs** for Veterans enrolled in the VA system of care. These programs are designed to assist Veterans to live and work as independently as possible in their respective communities. Participation in TSES vocational services cannot be used to deny or discontinue VA disability benefits. Payments received from Incentive Therapy and Compensated Work Therapy Sheltered Workshop and Transitional Work cannot be used to deny or discontinue SSI and/or SSDI payments and they are not subject to IRS taxes.

CWT/Transitional Work (CWT/TW) is vocational assessment program that operates in VA medical centers and/or local community business and industry. CWT/TW participants are matched to real life work assignments for a time-limited basis. Veterans are supervised by personnel of the sponsoring site, under the same job expectations experienced by non-CWT workers. Veterans participating in the CWT/TW program are not employees of either the Federal government or a host company and, as such, receive no traditional employee benefits. CWT/TW participants receive, at a minimum, the greater of Federal or state minimum wage for all hours worked. Approximately 40 percent of participants secure competitive employment at the time of discharge.

CWT/Supported Employment (CWT/SE) is a recovery-based intervention provided through an integrated partnership with the primary Mental Health treatment team. The employment is intended to be an extension of treatment to manage symptoms and advance recovery. CWT/SE consists of full or part-time competitive employment with extensive clinical supports to Veterans, and accommodations/supervision guidance to employers.

Other Initiatives include the adaption of SE evidence-based principles for specialty Therapeutic and Supported Employment Services programs for Veterans diagnosed with Spinal Cord Injury, Polytrauma, Traumatic Brain Injury, and/or Post Traumatic Stress Disorder. A list of CWT program sites can be found on the Location Page at http://www.cwt.va.gov.

Vocational Assistance is a set of assessment, guidance, counseling, or other related services that may be offered to groups or individuals. These services are designed to enable Veterans to realize skills, resources, attitudes and expectations needed to prepare for searching for employment, succeeding in the employment interview process, and succeeding in employment.
Compensated Work Therapy/Sheltered Workshop operates sheltered workshops at approximately 25 VA medical centers. CWT Sheltered Workshop is a pre-employment vocational activity that provides an opportunity for work hardening and assessment in a simulated work environment. Participating Veterans are paid the greater of Federal or state minimum wage on a piece rate basis.

Incentive Therapy (IT) is a pre-employment program that provides a limited work experience at VA medical centers for Veterans who are not actively seeking competitive employment and exhibit severe mental illness and/or physical impairments. IT services may consist of full- or part-time work with nominal remuneration limited to the maximum of one half of the Federal minimum wage.

Nursing Home Care

VA provides nursing home services to Veterans through three national programs: VA owned and operated Community Living Centers (CLC), State Veterans' Homes owned and operated by the states, and the community nursing home program. Each program has admission and eligibility criteria specific to the program. Nursing home care is available for enrolled Veterans who need nursing home care for a service-connected disability, or Veterans or who have a 70 percent or greater service-connected disability and Veterans with a rating of total disability based on individual unemployability. VA provided nursing home care for all other Veterans is based on available resources.

VA Community Living Centers: Community Living Centers (CLC) provide a dynamic array of short stay (less than 90 days) and long stay (91 days or more) services. Short stay services include but are not limited to skilled nursing, respite care, rehabilitation, hospice, and continuing care for Veterans awaiting placement in the community.

Long stay services include but are not limited to dementia care and continuing care to maintain the Veteran's level of functioning. Short stay and long stay services are available for Veterans who are enrolled in VA health care and require CLC services.

State Veterans' Home Program: State Veterans homes are owned and operated by the states. The states petition VA for grant dollars for a portion of the construction costs followed by a request for recognition as a state home. Once recognized, VA pays a portion of the per diem if the state meets VA standards. States establish eligibility criteria and determine services offered for short and long-term care. Specialized services offered are dependent upon the capability of the home to render them.

Community Nursing Home Program: VA health care facilities establish contracts with community nursing homes. The purpose of this program is to meet the nursing home needs of Veterans who require long-term nursing home care in their own community, close to their families and meet the enrollment and eligibility requirements.

Admission Criteria: The general criteria for nursing home placement in each of the three programs requires that a resident must be medically stable, i.e. not acutely ill, have sufficient functional deficits to require inpatient nursing home care, and be determined by an appropriate medical provider to need institutional nursing home care. Furthermore, the Veteran must meet the specific eligibility criteria for community living center care or the contract nursing home program and the eligibility criteria for the specific state Veterans home.

Home and Community Based Services: In addition to nursing home care, VA offers a variety of other long-term care services either directly or by contract with community-based agencies. Such services include adult day health care, respite care, geriatric evaluation and management, hospice and palliative care, skilled nursing and other skilled professional services at home, home health aide services, and home based primary care. Veterans receiving these services may be subject to a copay.

Emergency Medical Care in U.S. Non-VA Facilities
In the case of medical emergencies, VA may reimburse or pay for emergency non-VA medical care not previously authorized that is provided to certain eligible Veterans when VA or other federal facili-

ties are not feasibly available. This benefit may be dependent upon other conditions, such as notification to VA, the nature of treatment sought, the status of the Veteran, the presence of other health care insurance, and third party liability.

Because there are different regulatory requirements that may affect VA payment and Veteran liability for the cost of care, it is very important that the nearest VA medical facility to where emergency services are furnished be notified as soon as possible after emergency treatment is sought. If emergency inpatient services are required, VA will assist in transferring the Veteran to a Department facility, if available. Timely filing claim limitations apply. For additional information, contact the nearest VA medical facility. Please note that reimbursement criteria for Veterans living or traveling outside the United States fall under VA's Foreign Medical Program (FMP), and differ from the criteria for payment of emergency treatment received in the United States.

Foreign Medical Program

VA will provide reimbursement for medical services for service-connected disabilities or any disability associated with and found to be aggravating a service-connected disability for those Veterans living or traveling outside the United States. This program will also reimburse for the treatment of foreign medical services needed as part of an approved VA vocational rehabilitation program. Veterans living in the Philippines should register with the U.S. Veterans Affairs office in Pasay City, telephone 011-632-838-4566 or by email at manlopc.inqry@vba.va.gov. All other Veterans living or planning to travel outside the U.S. should register with the Denver Foreign Medical Program office, P.O. Box 469061, Denver, CO 80246-9061, USA; telephone 303-331-7590. For information visit: http://www.va.gov/hac/forbeneficiaries/fmp/fmp.asp

Some Veterans traveling or living overseas can telephone the Foreign Medical Program toll free from these countries: Germany 0800-1800-011; Australia 1800-354-965; Italy 800-782-655; United Kingdom (England and Scotland) 0800-032-7425; Mexico 001-877-345-8179; Japan 00531-13-0871; Costa Rica 0800-013-0759; and Spain 900-981-776. (Note: Veterans in Mexico or Costa Rica must first dial the United States country code.)

On occasion Veterans will ask to have prescriptions mailed outside the Unites States and its territories. VA Pharmacy Service will not ship medications or medical/surgical supply items outside of the Unites States or US Territories (Virgin Islands, Guam, American Samoa, and the Commonwealth of the Northern Mariana Islands). For Veterans registered with the Foreign Medical Program, prescription reimbursement is approved only for United States Food and Drug Administration (FDA) approved medications.

Within the United States and prior to travel abroad, VA facilities may opt to fill a Veteran patient's outpatient medications prior to the normal dispensing date in the event that a Veteran will be traveling and unable to obtain medications while abroad. This may be done on a limited basis and requires prior consultation with the Veteran patient's VA provider prior to dispensing.

Online Health Services

VA offers Veterans, Servicemembers, their dependents and caregivers their own personal health record through My HealtheVet, found at www.myhealth.va.gov.

My HealtheVet's free, online Personal Health Record is available 24/7 with Internet access. Those with an upgraded account (obtained by completing the one-time in-person authentication* process) can:

• Participate in secure messaging with VA health care team members
• View key portions of DoD military service information
• Get VA wellness reminders
• View VA appointments
• View VA lab results
• View VA allergies, adverse reactions and other key portions of their VA electronic health record.
• View their VA Comprehensive Care Document (CCD)

With My HealtheVet, Veterans can access trusted health information to better manage personal health care and learn about other VA benefits and services.

My HealtheVet helps Veterans partner with VA health care teams by providing tools to make shared, informed decisions. Simply follow the directions on the Website to register. VA patients registered on My HealtheVet can begin to refill VA medications online. Veterans can also use the VA Blue Button to view, print, or download the health data currently in their My HealtheVet account. Veterans can share this information with family, caregivers or others such as non-VA health care providers. It puts the Veteran in control of information stored in My HealtheVet. Accessible through My HealtheVet, VA Blue Button also provides Veterans who were discharged from military service after 1979 access to DoD Military Service Information. This information may include Military Occupational Specialty (MOS) codes, pay details, service dates, deployment, and retirement periods.

*To access the advanced My HealtheVet features, Veterans will need to get an upgraded account by completing a one-time process at their VA facility called in-person authentication. Visit My HealtheVet at www.myhealth.va.gov, register and learn more about in-person authentication plus the many features and tools available with Internet access. Veterans with questions should contact the My HealtheVet Coordinator at their VA facility.

Caregiver Programs and Services

VA has long supported Family Caregivers as vital partners in providing care worthy of the sacrifices by America's Veterans and Service-members. Each VA medical center has a Caregiver Support Program coordinated by a Caregiver Support Coordinator (CSC). The CSC coordinates Caregiver activities and serve as a resource expert for Veterans, their families and VA providers. Several programs are available for all Veteran Caregivers including:

In-Home and Community Based Care: Skilled home health care, homemaker/home health aide services, community adult day health care and Home Based Primary Care.

Respite Care: Designed to relieve the family Caregiver from the constant burden of caring for a chronically ill or disabled Veteran at home. Services can include in-home care, a short stay in an institutional setting or adult day health care.

Caregiver Education and Training Programs: VA currently provides multiple training opportunities which include pre-discharge care instruction and specialized Caregiver programs in multiple severe traumas such as Traumatic Brain Injury (TBI), Spinal Cord Injury/Disorders, and Blind Rehabilitation. VA has a Caregiver web site, www. caregiver.va.gov, which provides tools, resources, and information to

Family Caregivers.

Family Support Services: These support groups can be face-to-face or on the telephone. They include family counseling, spiritual and pastoral care, family leisure and recreational activities and temporary lodging in Fisher Houses.

Travel: VA's Comprehensive Assistance for Family Caregivers Program entitles the designated family caregiver to beneficiary travel benefits. These benefits include:
 • Transport, lodging, and subsistence for period of Caregiver
   training
 • Transport, lodging, and subsistence while traveling as Veteran's
   attendant to and from VA Healthcare as well as duration of
   care at VA or VA authorized facility.
 • Mileage or common carrier transport.
 • Lodging and/or subsistence at 50 percent of local federal
   employee rates

Other Benefits: VA provides durable medical equipment and pros-thetic and sensory aides to improve function, financial assistance with home modification to improve access and mobility, and trans-portation assistance for some Veterans to and from medical appoint-ments.

On May 5, 2010, the Caregivers and Veterans Omnibus Health Services Act of 2010 was signed into law. Title I of the Act will allow VA to provide unprecedented benefits to eligible Caregivers (a par-ent, spouse, child, step-family member, extended family member, or an individual who lives with the Veteran, but is not a family member) who support the Veterans who have given so much for this Nation. The law distinguishes between Veterans who incurred or aggravated a serious injury in the line of duty on or after Sept. 11, 2001 (post-9/11 Veterans), and those Veterans whose injuries were incurred prior to Sept. 11, 2001 (pre-9/11 Veterans).

The new services for this group include:
 • Monthly stipend based on the personal care needs of the Vet-
eran
 • Travel expenses, including lodging and per diem while accom-
panying Veterans undergoing care
 • Access to health care insurance through CHAMPVA if the

Caregiver is not already entitled to care or services under a health plan
- Mental health services and counseling
- Comprehensive VA Caregiver training provided by Easter Seals
- Respite care
- Appropriate caregiving instruction and training

Chapter 2
Service-connected Disabilities

Disability Compensation
Disability compensation is a monetary benefit paid to Veterans who are disabled by an injury or illness that was incurred or aggravated during active military service. These disabilities are considered to be service connected.

For additional details on types of disability claims and how to apply, go to http://benefits.va.gov/benefits/

Monthly disability compensation varies with the degree of disability and the number of eligible dependents. Veterans with certain severe disabilities may be eligible for additional special monthly compensation (SMC). Disability compensation benefits are not subject to federal or state income tax.

The payment of military retirement pay, disability severance pay and separation incentive payments, known as Special Separation Benefit (SSB) and Voluntary Separation Incentive (VSI), may affect the amount of VA compensation paid to disabled Veterans.

To be eligible for compensation, the Veteran must have been separated or discharged under conditions other than dishonorable.

Receiving Disability Benefit Payments
The Department of Treasury has mandated that all recurring federal benefits be administered through either Electronic Funds Transfer (EFT) or Direct Express® Debit MasterCard®. Compensation and pension beneficiaries can establish direct deposit through the Treasury's Go Direct helpline. Call toll-free 1-800-333-1795, or enroll

online at www.GoDirect.org.

Veterans also have the option of receiving their benefits via a pre-paid debit card, even if they do not have a bank account. There is no credit check, no minimum balance required, and basic services are free. To establish payments of federal benefits through Direct Express® Debit MasterCard® issued by Comerica Bank, call 1-888-213-1625 to enroll in the program.

2013 VA Disability Compensation Rates for Veterans	
Disability Rating	**Monthly Rate**
10 percent	$129
20 percent	$255
30 percent*	$395
40 percent*	$569
50 percent*	$810
60 percent*	$1,026
70 percent*	$1,293
80 percent*	$1,503
90 percent*	$1,689
100 percent*	$2,816

*Veterans with disability ratings of at least 30 percent are eligible for additional allowances for dependents, including spouses, minor children, children between the ages of 18 and 23 who are attending school, children who are permanently incapable of self-support because of a disability arising before age 18, and dependent parents. The additional amount depends on the disability rating and the number of dependents.

Additional Monetary Benefits for Eligible Military Retirees
Concurrent Retirement and Disability Pay (CRDP) is a Department of Defense (DoD) program that allows some individuals to receive both military retired pay and VA disability compensation. This dual receipt was prohibited until the CRDP program began on Jan. 1, 2004. CRDP is a "phase in" of benefits that gradually restores a retiree's VA disability offset. This means that an eligible person's retired pay will gradually increase each year until the phase in is complete in Jan. 2014.

Effective Jan. 1, 2005, Veterans rated 100 percent disabled by VA, including those receiving benefits at the 100 percent rate due to individual unemployability (IU), are entitled to full CRDP without being phased in.

Eligibility: To qualify for CRDP, Veterans must:
- Have a VA service-connected rating of 50 percent or greater, and:
- Be retired from military service based on longevity, including temporary Early Retirement Authority (TERA) retirees; or
- Be retired under Chapter 61 with 20 or more qualifying years of service; or
- Be retired from National Guard or Reserve service with 20 or more qualifying years; and
- Be eligible to receive retired pay (must be offset by VA payments).

Retirees do not need to apply for this benefit. Payment is coordinated between VA and the military pay center.

Combat-Related Special Compensation (CRSC) is a DoD program that provides tax-free monthly payments to eligible retired Veterans with combat-related disabilities. With CRSC, Veterans can receive both their military retirement pay and VA disability compensation for disabilities determined by the service department to be combat related.

Eligibility: To qualify for CRSC, Veterans must:
1. Be a military retiree.
2. Be entitled to and/or receiving military retired pay.
3. Have a compensable service-connected disability.

In addition, Veterans must be able to provide documentary evidence that their disabilities were the result of one of the following:
- Training that simulates war (e.g., exercises, field training)
- Hazardous duty (e.g., flight, diving, parachute duty)
- An instrumentality of war (e.g., combat vehicles, weapons)
- Armed conflict (e.g., gunshot wounds, Purple Heart)

Disabilities related to in-service exposure to hazards (e.g., Agent Orange, Gulf War illnesses, radiation exposure) for which VA awards compensation are considered combat-related for CRSC purposes.

For more information, visit www.defense.gov, or call the toll-free phone number for the Veteran's branch of service:

Army 1-866-281-3254, ,https://www.hrc.army.mil/site/crsc/index.html or e-mail at crsc.info@us.army.mil

Air Force 1-800-616-3775, http://www.retirees.af.mil/ or email at AFPC.DPPDC.AFCRSC@us.af.mil

Navy/Marine Corps 1-877-366-2772, www.donhq.navy.mil/corb/ CRSCB/combatrelated.htm or email at DoN_CRSC@navy.mil

Coast Guard 1-202-493-1735, http://www.uscg.mil/adm1/crsc.asp or email at Cassie.H.Sylvester@uscg.mil.

Disability Compensation for Presumptive Conditions
Certain chronic and tropical diseases (for example, multiple sclerosis, diabetes mellitus, and arthritis) may be service connected if the disease becomes at least 10 percent disabling within the applicable time limit following service. For a comprehensive list of these chronic diseases, see 38 CFR 3.309; for applicable time limits, see 38 CFR 3.307.

All Veterans who develop Amyotrophic Lateral Sclerosis (ALS), also known as Lou Gehrig's Disease, at any time after separation from service may be eligible for compensation for that disability. To be eligible, the Veteran must have served a minimum of 90 consecutive days of active service.

Prisoners of War: For former POWs who were imprisoned for any length of time, the following disabilities are presumed to be service connected if they become at least 10 percent disabling anytime after military service: psychosis, any of the anxiety states, dysthymic disorder, organic residuals of frostbite, post-traumatic osteoarthritis, atherosclerotic heart disease or hypertensive vascular disease and their complications, stroke and its complications, and, effective Oct.10, 2008, osteoporosis if the Veteran has post-traumatic stress disorder (PTSD).

For former POWs who were imprisoned for at least 30 days, the following conditions are also presumed to be service connected: avitaminosis, beriberi, chronic dysentery, helminthiasis, malnutrition (including optic atrophy associated with malnutrition), pellagra and/or other nutritional deficiencies, irritable bowel syndrome, peptic ulcer disease, peripheral neuropathy except where related to infectious causes, cirrhosis of the liver, and, effective Sept. 28, 2009, osteoporosis.

Veterans Exposed to Agent Orange and Other Herbicides: A Veteran who served in the Republic of Vietnam between Jan. 9, 1962, and May 7, 1975, is presumed to have been exposed to Agent Orange and other herbicides used in support of military operations. VA presumes the following diseases to be service-connected for such exposed Veterans: AL amyloidosis, chloracne or other acneform disease similar to chloracne, porphyria cutanea tarda, soft-tissue sarcoma (other than osteosarcoma, chondrosarcoma, Kaposi's sarcoma or mesothelioma), Hodgkin's disease, multiple myeloma, respiratory cancers (lung, bronchus, larynx, trachea), non-Hodgkin's lymphoma, prostate cancer, acute and subacute peripheral neuropathy, diabetes mellitus (Type 2), all chronic B-cell leukemias (including, but not limited to, hairy-cell leukemia and chronic lymphocytic leukemia), Parkinson's disease, and ischemic heart disease.

Veterans Exposed to Radiation: For Veterans who participated in radiation risk activities as defined in VA regulations while on active duty, active duty for training, or inactive duty training, the following conditions are presumed to be service connected: all forms of leukemia (except for chronic lymphocytic leukemia); cancer of the thyroid, breast, pharynx, esophagus, stomach, small intestine, pancreas, bile ducts, gall bladder, salivary gland, urinary tract (renal pelvis, ureter, urinary bladder and urethra), brain, bone, lung, colon, and ovary; bronchiolo-alveolar carcinoma; multiple myeloma; lymphomas (other than Hodgkin's disease), and primary liver cancer (except if cirrhosis or hepatitis B is indicated).

To determine service connection for other conditions or exposures not eligible for presumptive service connection, VA considers factors such as the amount of radiation exposure, duration of exposure, elapsed time between exposure and onset of the disease, gender and family history, age at time of exposure, the extent to which a non-service exposure could contribute to disease, and the relative sensitivity of exposed tissue.

Gulf War Veterans with Chronic Disabilities may receive disability compensation for chronic disabilities resulting from undiagnosed illnesses and/or medically unexplained chronic multi-symptom illnesses defined by a cluster of signs or symptoms. A disability is considered chronic if it has existed for at least six months.

The undiagnosed illness must have appeared either during active service in the Southwest Asia theater of operations during the Gulf War period of Aug. 2, 1990, to July 31, 1991, or to a degree of at least 10 percent at any time since then through Dec.31, 2016. This theater of operations includes Iraq, Kuwait, Saudi Arabia, the neutral zone between Iraq and Saudi Arabia, Bahrain, Qatar, the United Arab Emirates, Oman, the Gulf of Aden, the Gulf of Oman, the Persian Gulf, the Arabian Sea, the Red Sea, and the airspace above these locations.

Examples of symptoms of an undiagnosed illness and medically unexplained chronic multi-symptom illness defined by a cluster of signs and symptoms include: chronic fatigue syndrome, fibromyalgia, functional gastrointestinal disorders , fatigue, signs or symptoms involving the skin, headache, muscle pain, joint pain, neurological signs or symptoms, neuropsychological signs or symptoms, signs or symptoms involving the respiratory system (upper or lower), sleep disturbances, gastrointestinal signs or symptoms, cardiovascular signs or symptoms, abnormal weight loss, and menstrual disorders.

Presumptive service connection may be granted for the following infectious diseases if found compensable within a specific time period: Brucellosis, Campylobacter jejuni, Coxiella burnetti (Q fever), Malaria, Mycobacterium tuberculosis, Nontyphoid Salmonella, Shigella, Visceral leishmaniasis, and West Nile virus. Qualifying periods of service for these infectious diseases include active military, naval, or air service in the above stated Southwest Asia theater of operations during the Gulf War period of Aug. 2, 1990, until such time as the Gulf War is ended by Congressional action or Presidential proclamation; and active military, naval, or air service on or after Sept. 19, 2001, in Afghanistan.

Housing Grants for Disabled Veterans Certain Servicemembers and Veterans with service-connected disabilities may be entitled to a housing grant from VA to help build a new specially adapted house, to adapt a home they already own, or buy a house and modify it to meet their disability-related requirements. Eligible Veterans or Servicemembers may now receive up to three grants, with the total dollar amount of the grants not to exceed the maximum allowable. Previous grant recipients who had received assistance of less than the current maximum allowable may be eligible for an additional grant.

Specially Adapted Housing (SAH) Grant Eligibility for up to $64,960: VA may approve a grant of not more than 50 percent of the cost of building, buying, or adapting existing homes or paying to reduce indebtedness on a currently owned home that is being adapted, up to a maximum of $64,960. In certain instances, the full grant amount may be applied toward remodeling costs. Veterans and Servicemembers must be determined eligible to receive compensation for permanent and total service-connected disability due to one of the following:
1. Loss or loss of use of both lower extremities, which so affects the functions of balance or propulsion to preclude ambulating without the aid of braces, crutches, canes or a wheelchair.
   2. Loss or loss of use of both upper extremities at or above the elbow.
   3. Blindness in both eyes, having only light perception, plus loss or loss of use of one lower extremity.
   4. Loss or loss of use of one lower extremity together with (a) residuals of organic disease or injury, or (b) the loss or loss of use of one upper extremity which so affects the functions of balance or propulsion as to preclude locomotion without the use of braces, canes, crutches or a wheelchair.
   5. Severe burn injuries, which are defined as full thickness or subdermal burns that have resulted in contractures with limitation of motion of two or more extremities or of at least one extremity and the trunk.
   6. The loss, or loss of use of one or more lower extremities due to service
   on or after Sept. 11, 2001, which so affects the functions of balance or propulsion as to preclude ambulating without the aid of braces, crutches, canes, or a wheelchair.

Special Home Adaption (SHA) Grant: Eligibility for up to $12,992: VA may approve a benefit amount up to a maximum of $12,992, for the cost of necessary adaptations to a Servicemember's or Veteran's residence or to help him/her acquire a residence already adapted with special features for his/her disability, to purchase and adapt a home, or for adaptations to a family member's home in which they will reside.

To be eligible for this grant, Servicemembers and Veterans must be entitled to compensation for permanent and total service-connected disability due to one of the following:
  1. Blindness in both eyes with 20/200 visual acuity or less.
  2. Anatomical loss or loss of use of both hands.
  3. Severe burn injuries (see above).

Temporary Residence Adaptation (TRA): Eligible Veterans and Servicemembers who are temporarily residing in a home owned by a family member may also receive a TRA grant to help the Veteran or Servicemember adapt the family member's home to meet his or her special needs. Those eligible for a $64,960 grant would be permitted to use up to $28,515 and those eligible for a $12,992 grant would be permitted to use up to $5,092. Grant amounts are adjusted Oct.1 every year based on a cost-of-construction index. These adjustments will increase the grant amounts or leave them unchanged; grant amounts will not decrease. Under the Honoring America's Veterans and Caring for Camp Lejeune Families Act of 2012, TRA grant amounts will not count against SAH grant maximum amounts starting Aug. 6, 2013.

The property may be located outside the United States, in a country or political subdivision which allows individuals to have or acquire a beneficial property interest, and in which the Secretary of Veterans Affairs, in his or her discretion, has determined that it is reasonably practicable for the Secretary to provide assistance in acquiring specially adapted housing. For more information on SAH, visit http://www.benefits.va.gov/homeloans/sah.asp.

Supplemental Financing: Veterans and Servicemembers with available loan guaranty entitlement may also obtain a guaranteed loan or a direct loan from VA to supplement the grant to acquire a specially adapted home. Amounts with a guaranteed loan from a private lender will vary, but the maximum direct loan from VA is $33,000. Additional information about the Specially Adapted Housing Program is available at http://www.benefits.va.gov/homeloans/sah.asp.

Automobile Allowance: As of Oct. 1, 2012, Veterans and Service-members may be eligible for a one-time payment of not more than $19,505 toward the purchase of an automobile or other conveyance if they have service-connected loss or permanent loss of use of one or both hands or feet, or permanent impairment of vision of both eyes to a certain degree.

They may also be eligible for adaptive equipment, and for repair, replacement, or reinstallation required because of disability or for the safe operation of a vehicle purchased with VA assistance. To apply, contact a VA regional office at 1-800-827-1000 or the nearest VA health care facility.

Clothing Allowance: Any Veteran who has service-connected disabilities that require a prosthetic or orthopedic appliances may receive clothing allowances. This allowance is also available to any Veteran whose service-connected skin condition requires prescribed medication that irreparably damages outer garments. To apply, contact the prosthetic representative at the nearest VA medical center.

Allowance for Aid and Attendance or Housebound Veterans
A Veteran who is determined by VA to be in need of the regular aid and attendance of another person, or a Veteran who is permanently housebound, may be entitled to additional disability compensation or pension payments. A Veteran evaluated at 30 percent or more disabled is entitled to receive an additional payment for a spouse who is in need of the aid and attendance of another person.

Chapter 3
VR&E

Vocational Rehabilitation and Employment (VR&E): sometimes referred to as the Chapter 31 program. VR&E provides services to eligible Servicemembers and Veterans with service-connected disabilities to help them prepare for, obtain, and maintain suitable employment or achieve independence in daily living. Additional information is available at www.vetsuccess.gov.

Eligibility for Veterans: A Veteran must have a VA service-connected disability rated at least 20 percent with an employment handicap, or rated 10 percent with a serious employment handicap, and be discharged or released from military service under other than dishonorable conditions.

Eligibility for Servicemembers: Servicemembers are eligible to apply if they expect to receive an honorable discharge upon separation from active duty, obtain a rating of 20 percent percent or more from VA, obtain a proposed Disability Evaluation System (DES) rating of 20 percent percent or more from VA, or obtain a referral to a Physical Evaluation Board (PEB) through the Integrated Disability Evaluation System (IDES).

Entitlement: A Vocational Rehabilitation Counselor (VRC) works with the Veteran to determine if an employment handicap exists. An employment handicap exists if a Veteran's service- connected disability impairs his/her ability to prepare for, obtain, and maintain suitable career employment. After an entitlement decision is made, the Veteran and VRC work together to develop a rehabilitation plan. The rehabilitation plan outlines the rehabilitation services to be provided.

Services: Based on their individualized needs, Veterans work with a VRC to select one of five vocational tracks of services. If a program of training is selected, the VA pays the cost of the approved training and services (except those coordinated through other providers) that are included in an individual's rehabilitation plan, including subsistence allowance.

VR&E's five tracks of services are:

Reemployment with Previous Employer: For individuals who are separating from active duty or in the National Guard or Reserves and are returning to work for their previous employer.

Rapid Access to Employment: For individuals who either wish to obtain employment soon after separation or who already have the necessary skills to be competitive in the job market in an appropriate occupation.

Self-Employment: For individuals who have limited access to traditional employment, need flexible work schedules, or who require more accommodation in the work environment due to their disabling conditions or other life circumstances.

Employment Through Long-Term Services: For individuals who need specialized training and/or education to obtain and maintain suitable employment.

Independent Living Services: For Veterans who are not currently able to work and need rehabilitation services to live more independently.

Length of a Rehabilitation Program: The basic period of eligibility in which VR&E benefits may be used is 12 years from the latter of the following: 1). A Veteran's date of separation from active military service, or 2). The date VA first notified a Veteran that he/she have a compensable service-connected disability. Depending on the length of program needed, Veterans may be provided up to 48 months of full-time services or the part-time equivalent. Rehabilitation plans that only provide services to improve independence in daily living are limited to 30 months. These limitations may be extended in certain circumstances.

Intergrated Disability Evaluation System (IDES): VR&E is providing earlier access to VR&E benefits to wounded, ill or injured Servicemembers pending a medical separation from military service. Vocational Rehabilitation Counselors are assigned to military installations hosting an IDES site and provide VR&E services to assist Servicemembers in the transition from active-duty to entering the labor market in viable careers.

Current locations include: Joint Base Elmendorf-Richardson, Ft. Wainwright, Ft. Benning, Ft. Gordon, Robins AFB, Ft. Meade, Ft. Drum, BeauFt. NH, Ft. Jackson, Ft. Carson, Tripler AMC, Pearl Harbor NH, San Antonio JB (Sam Houston), Ft. Irwin, Ft. Knox, White-River Junction, Pensacola NH, Ft. Rucker, Redstone Arsenal, Ft. Sill, Sheppard AFB, Ft. Campbell, Ft. Polk, Travis AFB, Ft. Huachuca, Nellis AFB, Ft. Eustis, Portsmouth NMC, Ft. Lee, Langley JB, San Diego Navy Medical Center (Balboa), Ft. Lewis, Kitsap Naval Base, Fairchild AFB, Ft. Lewis (JB Lewis McChord), Ft. Leonard Wood, Jacksonville NH, Ft. Bliss, Ft. Hood, Bethesda NNMC/Walter Reed AMC, Andrews AFB, Ft. Belvoir, MCB Quantico, Ft. Riley, Camp Lejuene, Ft. Bragg, Seymour-Johnson AFB, and Cherry Point NH.

VetSuccess.gov: See page 57.

Work-Study Program: Refer to Chapter 5, "Education and Training"

Educational and Vocational Counseling Services: Refer to Chapter 10, "Transition Assistance"

Dependents and Survivors Educational Assistance: Refer to Chapter 12, "Dependents and Survivors Benefits"

Fiduciary Program: The fiduciary program provides oversight of VA's most vulnerable beneficiaries who are unable to manage their VA benefits because of injury, disease, the infirmities of advanced age, or being under 18 years of age. VA appoints fiduciaries who manage VA benefits for these beneficiaries and conducts oversight of VA-appointed fiduciaries to ensure that they are meeting the needs of the beneficiaries they serve.

VA closely monitors fiduciaries for compliance with program responsibilities to ensure that VA benefits are being used for the purpose of meeting the needs, security, and comfort of beneficiaries and their dependents. In deciding who should act as fiduciary for a beneficiary, VA will always select the most effective and least restrictive fiduciary arrangement.

This means that VA will first consider whether the beneficiary can manage his/her VA benefits with limited supervision. VA will consider the choice of the beneficiary as well as any family, friends and caregivers who are qualified and willing to provide fiduciary services for the beneficiary without a fee.

As a last resort, VA will consider appointment of a paid fiduciary. For more information about VA's fiduciary program, please visit our website at http://benefits.va.gov/fiduciary/index.asp.

Vocational Rehabilitation and Employment Subsistence Allowance: In some cases, a Veteran may require additional education or training to become employable. A subsistence allowance is paid each month during training and is based on the rate of attendance (full-time or part-time), the number of dependents, and the type of training.

Veterans who are eligible for both VR&E services and Post-9/11 GI Bill benefits may elect a special subsistence allowance that is based on the monthly basic allowance for housing paid to active duty military. The monthly amount varies depending on the ZIP code of the training facility and is usually greater than the following regular subsistence allowance rates that are available to Veterans with no Post-9/11 GI Bill eligibility who are using VR&E benefits.

Active-duty Servicemembers are not eligible for subsistence allowance until after Release from Active Duty date (RAD). 2012.

VR&E Subsistence Allowance Rates as of Oct. 1, 2012

Training	Time	No dependents	One dependent	Two dependents	Each Additional dependent
Institutional*	Full-Time	$585.11	$725.78	$855.28	$62.34
	3/4-Time	$439.64	$545.13	$639.45	$47.94
	1/2-Time	$294.17	$364.47	$428.42	$31.99
Farm Co-op Apprentice OJT**	Full-Time	$511.58	$618.65	$713.00	$46.38
Extended Evaluation Services in Rehab Facility	Full-Time	$585.11	$725.78	$855.28	$62.34
	3/4-Time	$439.64	$545.13	$639.45	$47.94
	1/2-Time	$294.17	$364.47	$428.42	$31.99
	1/4-Time	$147.06	$182.25	$214.21	$15.95
Independ. Living	Full-Time	$585.11	$725.78	$855.28	$62.34
	3/4-Time	$439.64	$545.13	$639.45	$47.94
	1/2-Time	$294.17	$364.47	$428.42	$31.99

For VR&E Training Programs Subsistence Allowance Rates, please go to http://www.vba.va.gov/bln/vre/sa.htm.

Chapter 4
VA Pensions

Eligibility for Veterans Pension
Low-income wartime Veterans may qualify for pension if they meet certain service, income and net worth limits set by law; are age 65 or older, permanently and totally disabled, a patient in a nursing home receiving skilled nursing care, receiving Social Security Disability Insurance, or receiving Supplemental Security Income. Generally, a Veteran must have at least 90 days of active duty service, with at least one day during a VA recognized wartime period. The 90-day active service requirement does not apply to Veterans discharged from the military due to a service-connected disability. (Veterans may have to meet longer minimum periods of active duty if they entered active duty on or after Sept. 8, 1980, or, if they were officers who entered active duty on or after Oct. 16, 1981.) The Veteran's discharge must have been under conditions other than dishonorable and the disability must be for reasons other than the Veteran's own willful misconduct.

Payments are made to bring the Veteran's total income, including other retirement or Social Security income, to a level set by Congress. Unreimbursed medical expenses may reduce countable income for VA purposes.

Protected Pension: Pension beneficiaries, who were receiving a VA pension on December 31, 1978, and do not wish to elect the Improved Pension, will continue to receive the pension rate received on that date. This rate generally continues as long as the beneficiary's income remains within established limits, or net worth does not bar payment, and the beneficiary does not lose any dependents.

Beneficiaries must continue to meet basic eligibility factors, such as permanent and total disability for Veterans. VA must adjust rates for other reasons, such as a Veteran's hospitalization in a VA facility.

Medal of Honor Pension: VA administers a pension benefit to recipients of the Medal of Honor. This entitlement is not based on income level or need. Congress set the monthly pension at $1,259 for 2013.

Veterans Pension: Congress establishes the maximum annual Veterans Pension rates. Payments are reduced by the amount of countable income of the Veteran, spouse, and dependent children. When a Veteran without a spouse or a child is furnished nursing home or domiciliary care by VA, the pension is reduced to an amount not to exceed $90 per month after three calendar months of care. The reduction may be delayed if nursing-home care is being continued to provide the Veteran with rehabilitation services.

Aid and Attendance and Housebound Benefits (Special Monthly Pension): Veterans and surviving spouses who are eligible for VA pensions are eligible for higher maximum pension rates if they qualify for aid and attendance or housebound benefits. An eligible individual may qualify if he or she requires the regular aid of another person in order to perform personal functions required in everyday living, or is bedridden, a patient in a nursing home due to mental or physical incapacity, blind, or permanently and substantially confined to his/her immediate premises because of a disability.

Veterans and surviving spouses who are ineligible for basic pension based on annual income may still be eligible for VA Pension if they are eligible for aid and attendance or housebound benefits because a higher income limit applies. In addition, unreimbursed medical expenses for nursing home or home-health care may be used to reduce countable annual income, which may result in a higher pension benefit.

Claimants may apply for aid and attendance or housebound benefits by completing VA Form 21-2680 (available through www.va.gov). Claimants may also write to the nearest VA regional office and include copies of any evidence, preferably a report from an attending physician or a nursing home, validating the need for aid and attendance or housebound care. The report should be in sufficient detail to determine whether there is disease or injury producing physical or mental impairment, loss of coordination, or conditions affecting the ability to dress and undress, to feed oneself, to attend to sanitary needs, and to keep oneself ordinarily clean and presentable. In addition, VA may need to determine whether the claimant is confined to the home or immediate premises.

VA also pays a special $90 monthly rate to pension-eligible Veterans or surviving spouses with no dependents who receive Medicaid-cov-

ered nursing home care. These funds are available for the beneficiary's personal use and may not be used to offset the cost of his or
her care.

2012 VA Improved Pension - Veterans Rates	
Status of Veteran's Family Situation and Caretaking Needs	**Maximum Annual Rate**
Veteran without dependents	$12,465
Veteran with one dependent	$16,324
Veteran permanently housebound, no dependents	$15,233
Veteran permanently housebound, one dependent	$19,093
Veteran needing regular aid and attendance, no dependents	$20,795
Veteran needing regular aid and attendance, one dependent	$24,652
Two Veterans married to one another	$16,324
Increase for each additional dependent child	$2,129

* Additional information can be found in the Pension Benefits section at www.
benefits.va.gov/pension/

Chapter 5
Education and Training

This chapter provides a summary of VA educational and training benefits. Additional information can be found at www.gibill.va.gov/ or by calling 1-888-GI-BILL-1 (1-888-442-4551).

Post – 9/11 GI Bill

Eligibility: The Post- 9/11 GI Bill is an education benefit program for Servicemembers and Veterans who served on active duty after Sept. 10, 2001. Benefits are payable for training pursued on or after Aug. 1, 2009. No payments can be made under this program for training pursued before that date.

To be eligible, the Servicemember or Veteran must serve at least 90 aggregate days on active duty after Sept. 10, 2001, and remain on active duty or be honorably discharged. Active duty includes active service performed by National Guard members under title 32 U.S.C. for the purposes of organizing, administering, recruiting, instructing, or training the National Guard; or under section 502(f) for the purpose of responding to a national emergency. Veterans may also be eligible if they were honorably discharged from active duty for a service-connected disability after serving 30 continuous days after Sept. 10, 2001. Generally, Servicemembers or Veterans may receive up to 36 months of entitlement under the Post-9/11 GI Bill.

Eligibility for benefits expires 15 years from the last period of active duty of at least 90 consecutive days. If released for a service-connected disability after at least 30 days of continuous service, eligibility ends 15 years from when the member is released for the service-connected disability. If, on Aug.1, 2009, the Servicemember or Veteran is eligible for the Montgomery GI Bill; the Montgomery GI Bill – Selected Reserve; or the Reserve Educational Assistance Program, and qualifies for the Post-9/11 GI Bill, an irrevocable election must be made to receive benefits under the Post-9/11 GI Bill.
In most instances, once the election to receive benefits under the Post-9/11 GI Bill is made, the individual will no longer be eligible to receive benefits under the relinquished program.

Based on the length of active duty service, eligible participants are entitled to receive a percentage of the following:
1. Cost of in-state tuition and fees at public institutions and for the 2011-2012 academic year, up to $17,500 towards tuition and fee costs at private and foreign institutions (paid directly to the school);
2. Monthly housing allowance equal to the basic allowance for housing payable to a military E-5 with dependents, in the same Zip code as the primary school (paid directly to the Servicemember, Veteran, or eligible dependents);
3. Yearly books and supplies stipend of up to $1,000 per year (paid directly to the Servicemember, Veteran, or eligible dependents); and
4. A one-time payment of $500 paid to certain individuals relocating from highly rural areas.

* The housing allowance is not payable to individuals pursuing training at half time or less.

Approved training under the Post-9/11 GI Bill includes graduate and undergraduate degrees, vocational/technical training, on-the-job training, flight training, correspondence training, licensing and national testing programs, and tutorial assistance.

Individuals serving an aggregate period of active duty after Sept. 10, 2001 can receive the following percentages based on length of service:

Active Duty Service	Maximum Benefit
At least 36 months	100 percent
At least 30 continuous days and discharged due to service-connected disability	100 percent
At least 30 months < 36 months (1)	90 percent
At least 24 months < 30 months (1)	80 percent (3)
At least 18 months < 24 months (2)	70 percent
At least 12 months < 18 months (2)	60 percent
At least 6 months < 12 months (2)	50 percent
At least 90 days < 6 months (2)	40 percent

(1) Includes service on active duty in entry level and skill training. (2) Excludes service on active duty in entry level and skill training. (3) If the

individual would only qualify at the 70 percent level when service on active duty in entry level and skill training is excluded, then VA can only pay at the 70 percent level.

The Yellow Ribbon G.I. Education Enhancement Program was enacted to potentially assist eligible individuals with payment of their tuition and fees in instances where costs exceed the in-state tuition charges at a public institution or the national maximum payable at private and foreign institutions. To be eligible, the student must be: a Veteran receiving benefits at the 100 percent benefit rate payable, a transfer-of-entitlement-eligible dependent child, or a transfer-of-entitlement eligible spouse of a Veteran.

The school of attendance must have accepted VA's invitation to participate in the program, state how much student tuition will be waived (up to 50 percent) and how many participants will be accepted into the program during the current academic year. VA will match the school's percentage (up to 50 percent) to reduce or eliminate out-of-pocket costs for eligible participants.

Transfer of Entitlement (TOE): DoD may offer members of the Armed Forces on or after Aug.1, 2009, the opportunity to transfer benefits to a spouse or dependent children. DoD and the military services must approve all requests for this benefit. Members of the Armed Forces approved for the TOE may only transfer any unused portion of their Post-9/11 GI Bill benefits while a member of the Armed Forces, subject to their period of eligibility.

Marine Gunnery Sergeant John David Fry Scholarship: This scholarship entitles children of those who die in the line of duty on or after Sept. 11, 2001, to use Post-9/11 GI Bill benefits.

Eligible children:
- are entitled to 36 months of benefits at the 100 percent level
- have 15 years to use the benefit beginning on their 18th birthday
- may use the benefit until their 33rd birthday
- are not eligible for the Yellow Ribbon Program

Restoring GI Bill Fairness Act of 2011
The Restoring GI Bill Fairness Act of 2011 amended the Post-9/11 GI Bill. The provisions of the bill are applicable to training pursued under

the Post-9/11 GI Bill that began on or after Aug. 1, 2011.

The legislation authorizes VA to pay more than the national maximum set for private schools (currently $17,500 or the appropriately reduced amount based on eligibility percentage) in tuition and fees under the Post-9/11 GI Bill for certain students attending private colleges and universities in seven states - Arizona, Michigan, New Hampshire, New York, Pennsylvania, South Carolina and Texas.

To qualify for the increased payment (also referred to as the "grand-fathered" tuition and fee amount), students must have been enrolled in the same college or university since Jan. 4, 2011, and have been enrolled in a program for which the combined amount of tuition and fees for full-time attendance during the 2010-2011 academic year exceeded $17,500.

VOW to Hire Heroes Act of 2011

Included in this new law is the Veterans Retraining Assistance Program (VRAP) for unemployed Veterans. VA and the Department of Labor (DoL) rolled out this new program on July 1, 2012. The program provides retraining for Veterans hardest hit by current economic conditions.

VRAP offers 12 months of training assistance to unemployed Veterans. To qualify, a Veteran must:
• Be at least 35, but no more than 60 years old
• Be unemployed (as determined by DoL)
• Have an other than dishonorable discharge
• Not be eligible for any other VA education benefit program (e.g., the Post-9/11 GI Bill, Montgomery GI Bill, Vocational Rehabilitation and Employment assistance)
• Not be in receipt of VA compensation due to unemployability
• Not be enrolled in a federal or state job-training program

The program is limited to 54,000 participants from Oct. 1, 2012, through March 31, 2014. Participants may receive up to 12 months of assistance at the full-time payment rate under the Montgomery GI Bill–Active Duty program (currently $1,564 per month). Applications will be submitted through DoL and benefits paid by VA. DoL provides employment assistance to every Veteran who participates upon completion of their program.

Participants must be enrolled in a VA-approved program of education offered by a community college or technical school. The program must lead to an associate degree, non-college degree, or a certification, and train the Veteran for a high-demand occupation.

More details will be available at www.gibill.va.gov and on VA's Facebook, which are updated regularly.

VetSuccess on Campus: is designed to provide on-campus benefits assistance and readjustment counseling to assist Veterans in completing their college educations and entering the labor market in viable careers. Under this program, a full-time, experienced Vocational Rehabilitation Counselor and a part-time Vet Center Outreach

Coordinator are assigned at each campus to provide VA benefits outreach, support, and assistance to ensure their health, educational, and benefit needs are met.
Current locations include Cleveland State University, Community College of Rhode Island, Rhode Island College, University of Maryland University College, Western Michigan University, Kalamazoo Valley Community College, Kellogg Community College, Eastern Michigan University, University of Michigan - Ann Arbor, Washtenaw Community College, University of South Florida, Middle Tennessee State University, Eastern Kentucky University, Norfolk State University, Tidewater Community College, Tidewater Community College – Chesapeake, Tidewater Community College – Portsmouth, Tidewater Community College - Virginia Beach, Tarrant County College District - South Campus, Tarrant County College District - Northeast Campus, Texas A&M University - Central Texas, Sam Houston State University, University of Texas-San Antonio, Arizona State University, Boise State University, Salt Lake Community College, University of Utah, Portland State University, San Diego State University, University of Alaska –Anchorage, Central New Mexico Community College, and University of New Mexico.

Educational and Vocational Counseling Services: Refer to Chapter 10, "Transition Assistance," for detailed information on available services.

Montgomery GI Bill
Eligibility: VA educational benefits may be used while the Servicemember is on active duty or after the Servicemember's separation from active duty with a fully honorable military discharge. Discharges

"under honorable conditions" and "general" discharges do not establish eligibility.

Eligibility generally expires 10 years after the Servicemember's discharge. However, there are exceptions for disability, re-entering active duty, and upgraded discharges. All participants must have a high school diploma, equivalency certificate, or have completed 12 hours toward a college degree before applying for benefits.

Previously, Servicemembers had to meet the high school requirement before they completed their initial active duty obligation. Those who did not may now meet the requirement and reapply for benefits. If eligible, they must use their benefits within 10 years from the date of last discharge from active duty.

Additionally, every Veteran must establish eligibility under one of four categories.

Category 1: Service after June 30, 1985
For Veterans who entered active duty for the first time after June 30, 1985, did not decline MGIB in writing, and had their military pay reduced by $100 a month for 12 months. Servicemembers can apply after completing two continuous years of service. Veterans must have completed three continuous years of active duty, or two continuous years of active duty if they first signed up for less than three years or have an obligation to serve four years in the Selected Reserve (the 2x4 program) and enter the Selected Reserve within one year of discharge.

Servicemembers or Veterans who received a commission as a result of graduation from a service academy or completion of an ROTC scholarship are not eligible under Category 1 unless they received their commission:
    1. After becoming eligible for MGIB benefits (including completing the minimum service requirements for the initial period of active duty); or
    2. After Sept. 30, 1996, and received less than $3,400 during any one year under ROTC scholarship.

Servicemembers or Veterans who declined MGIB because they received repayment from the military for education loans are also ineligible under Category 1. If they did not decline MGIB and received loan repayments, the months served to repay the loans will be deducted from their entitlement.

Early Separation from Military Service: Servicemembers who did not complete the required period of military service may be eligible under:

Category 1: If discharged for one of the following:
1. Convenience of the government—with 30 continuous months of service for an obligation of three or more years, or 20 continuous months of service for an obligation of less than three years
2. Service-connected disability
3. Hardship
4. A medical condition diagnosed prior to joining the military
5. A condition that interfered with performance of duty and did not result from misconduct
6. A reduction in force (in most cases)
7. Sole Survivorship (if discharged after 9/11/01)

Category 2: Vietnam Era GI Bill Conversion
For Veterans who had remaining entitlement under the Vietnam Era GI Bill on Dec. 31, 1989, and served on active duty for any number of days during the period Oct. 19, 1984, to June 30, 1985, for at least three continuous years beginning on July 1, 1985; or at least two continuous years of active duty beginning on July 1, 1985, followed by four years in the Selected Reserve beginning within one year of release from active duty.

Veterans not on active duty on Oct. 19, 1984, may be eligible under Category 2 if they served three continuous years on active duty beginning on or after July 1, 1985, or two continuous years of active duty at any time followed by four continuous years in the Selected Reserve beginning within one year of release from active duty.

Veterans are barred from eligibility under Category 2 if they received a commission after Dec. 31, 1976, as a result of graduation from a service academy or completion of an ROTC scholarship.

However, such a commission is not disqualifying if they received the commission after becoming eligible for MGIB benefits, or received the commission after Sept. 30, 1996, and received less than $3,400 during any one year under ROTC scholarship.

Category 3: Involuntary Separation/Special Separation
For Veterans who meet one of the following requirements:
1. Elected MGIB before being involuntarily separated; or
2. were voluntarily separated under the Voluntary Separation Incentive or the Special Separation Benefit program, elected MGIB benefits before being separated, and had military pay reduced by $1,200 before discharge.

Category 4: Veterans Educational Assistance Program
For Veterans who participated in the Veterans Educational Assistance Program (VEAP) and:
1. Served on active duty on Oct. 9, 1996.
2. Participated in VEAP and contributed money to an account.
3. Elected MGIB by Oct. 9, 1997, and paid $1,200.

Veterans who participated in VEAP on or before Oct. 9, 1996, may also be eligible even if they did not deposit money in a VEAP account if they served on active duty from Oct. 9, 1996, through April 1, 2000, elected MGIB by Oct. 31, 2001, and contributed $2,700 to MGIB.

Certain National Guard Servicemembers may also qualify under Category 4 if they:
1. Served for the first time on full-time active duty in the National Guard between June 30, 1985, and Nov. 29, 1989, and had no previous active duty service.
2. Elected MGIB during the nine-month window ending on July 9, 1997; and
3. Paid $1,200.

Payments: Effective Oct. 1, 2012, the rate for full-time training in college, technical or vocational school is $1,564 a month for those who served three years or more or two years plus four years in the Selected Reserve. For those who served less than three years, the monthly rate is $1,270

Benefits are reduced for part-time training. Payments for other types of training follow different rules. VA will pay an additional amount, called a "kicker" or "college fund," if directed by DoD. Visit www.gibill. va.gov for more information. The maximum number of months Veterans can receive payments is 36 months at the full-time rate or the part-time equivalent.

The following groups qualify for the maximum: Veterans who served the required length of active duty, Veterans with an obligation of three years or more who were separated early for the convenience of the government and served 30 continuous months, and Veterans with an obligation of less than three years who were separated early for the convenience of the government and served 20 continuous months.

Types of Training Available:
1. Courses at colleges and universities leading to associate, bachelor or graduate degrees, including accredited independent study offered through distance education.
2. Courses leading to a certificate or diploma from business, technical or vocational schools.
3. Apprenticeship or on-the-job training for those not on active duty, including self-employment training begun on or after June 16, 2004, for ownership or operation of a franchise
4. Correspondence courses, under certain conditions.
5. Flight training, if the Veteran holds a private pilot's license upon beginning the training and meets the medical requirements.
6. State-approved teacher certification programs.
7. Preparatory courses necessary for admission to a college or graduate school.
8. License and certification tests approved for Veterans.
9. Entrepreneurship training courses to create or expand small businesses.
10. Tuition assistance using MGIB as "Top-Up" (active duty Servicemembers).

Accelerated payments for certain high-cost programs are authorized.

Work-Study Program: Participants who train at the three-quarter or full-time rate may be eligible for a work-study program in which they work for VA and receive hourly wages. Students under the work-study program must be supervised by a VA employee, and all duties performed must relate to VA. The types of work allowed include:

Working in Veterans-related position at schools or other training facilities.

Providing hospital or domiciliary care at a state home.
Working at national or state Veterans' cemeteries.
Various jobs within any VA facility.
Providing assistance in obtaining a benefit under title 38 U.S.C. at a state Veterans agency.
Assisting in the administration of chapters 1606 or 1607 of title 10 U.S.C. at a Department of Defense, Coast Guard, or National Guard facility.
Working in a Center for Excellence for Veterans Student Success.

Educational and Vocational Counseling Services: Refer to Chapter 10, "Transition Assistance", for detailed information on available services.

Veterans' Educational Assistance Program

Eligibility: Active duty personnel could participate in the Veterans' Educational Assistance Program (VEAP) if they entered active duty for the first time after Dec. 31, 1976, and before July 1, 1985, and made a contribution prior to April 1, 1987.

The maximum contribution is $2,700. Active duty participants may make a lump-sum contribution to their VEAP account. For more information, visit www.gibill.va.gov.

Servicemembers who participated in VEAP are eligible to receive benefits while on active duty if:
1. At least three months of contributions are available, except for high school or elementary, in which only one month is needed.
2. And they enlisted for the first time after Sept. 7, 1980, and completed 24 months of their first period of active duty.

Servicemembers must receive a discharge under conditions other than dishonorable for the qualifying period of service. Servicemembers who enlisted for the first time after Sept. 7, 1980, or entered active duty as an officer or enlistee after Oct. 16, 1981, must have completed 24 continuous months of active duty, unless they meet a qualifying exception.

Eligibility generally expires 10 years from release from active duty, but can be extended under special circumstances.

Payments: DoD will match contributions at the rate of $2 for every $1 put into the fund and may make additional contributions, or "kickers," as necessary. For training in college, vocational or technical schools, the payment amount depends on the type and hours of training pursued. The maximum amount is $300 a month for full-time training.

Training, Work-Study, Counseling: VEAP participants may receive the same training, work-study benefits and counseling as provided under the MGIB with the exception of preparatory courses.

Employment Services

VetSuccess.gov

The Department of Veterans Affairs provides Veterans with employment and transition assistance through the VetSuccess.gov Website. VetSuccess.gov is a Veteran-centric tool, providing a number of employment and transition resources. Veterans can access VetSuccess.gov to:

    Browse job listings
    Post resumes
    Apply for positions

Employers can use VetSuccess.gov to hire Veterans by posting job openings or by searching a database of over 25,000 Veteran resumes. VetSuccess.gov provides links to millions of jobs on the VetCentral site and the Veterans Job Bank search engine, and links Veterans to Indeed, Google, Simply Hired, and other job search engines. Veterans may also apply for VA benefits, including Vocational Rehabilitation and Employment, through the site.

Veterans, Servicemembers, and their families can also access a variety of interactive tools and information available throughout the Veteran lifecycle from transition to college, career, retirement, and family life.

Servicemembers and Veterans with Disabilities

Eligible Veterans or Servicemembers with disabilities who require assistance with obtaining and maintaining employment may receive services through the Vocational Rehabilitation & Employment (VR&E) program (see chapter 2 for eligibility information). VR&E staff assists Veterans and Servicemembers with achieving their employment goals by providing job development and placement services, which include: on-the-job training, job-seeking skills, resume development, interviewing skills and direct placement. VR&E has partnerships with federal, state and private agencies to provide direct placement of Veterans or Servicemembers. VR&E can assist with placement using the following resources:

On the Job Training Program: Employers hire Veterans at an apprentice wage, and VR&E supplements the salary up the journey-man wage (up to maximum allowable under OJT). As the Veterans progress through training, the employers begin to pay more of the salary until the Veterans reach journeyman level and the employers are paying the entire salary. VR&E will also pay for any necessary tools. Employers are also eligible for a federal tax credit for hiring an individual who participated in a vocational rehabilitation program.

Non-Paid Work Experience: The Non-Paid Work Experience (NPWE) program provides eligible Veterans the opportunity to obtain training and practical job experience concurrently. This program is ideal for Veterans or Servicemembers who have a clearly estab-lished career goal, and who learn easily in a hands-on environment. This program is also well suited for Veterans who are having difficul-ties obtaining employment due to lack of work experience. NPWE program may be established in a federal, state, or local (i.e. city, town, school district) government agencies only. The employer may hire the Veteran at any point during the NPWE.

Special Employer Incentive: The Special Employer Incentive (SEI) program is for eligible Veterans who face challenges in obtaining employment. Veterans approved to participate in the SEI program are hired by participating employers and employment is expected to continue following successful completion of the program. Employ-ers may be provided this incentive to hire Veterans. If approved, the employer will receive reimbursement for up to 50 percent of the Veteran's salary during the SEI program, which can last up to six months.

Chapter 6
Home Loan Guaranty

VA home loan guaranties are issued to help eligible Servicemembers, Veterans, Reservists, National Guard and certain unmarried surviving spouses obtain homes, condominiums, and manufactured homes, and to refinance loans. For additional information or to obtain VA loan guaranty forms, visit http://www.benefits.va.gov/homeloans/.

Loan Uses: A VA guaranty helps protect lenders from loss if the borrower fails to repay the loan. It can be used to obtain a loan to:
1. Buy or build a home.
2. Buy a residential condominium unit.
3. Repair, alter, or improve a residence owned by the Veteran and occupied as a home.
4. Refinance an existing home loan.
5. Buy a manufactured home and/or lot.
6. Install a solar heating or cooling system or other energy-efficient improvements.

Eligibility: In addition to the periods of eligibility and conditions of service requirements, applicants must have a good credit rating, sufficient income, a valid Certificate of Eligibility (COE), and agree to live in the property in order to be approved by a lender for a VA home loan.

Lenders can apply for a COE online through the Veterans Information Portal (https://vip.vba.va.gov/portal/VBAH/Home). Active duty Servicemembers and Veterans can also apply online at http://www. ebenefits.va.gov. Although it's preferable to apply electronically, it is possible to apply for a COE using VA Form 26-1880, Request for Certificate of Eligibility.

In applying for a hard-copy COE from the VA Eligibility Center using VA Form 26-1880, it is typically necessary that the eligible Veteran present a copy of his/her report of discharge or DD Form 214, Certificate of Release or Discharge from Active Duty, or other adequate substitute evidence to VA. An eligible active duty Servicemember should obtain and submit to the VA Eligibility Center a statement of service signed by an appropriate military official. A completed VA Form 26-1880 and any associated documentation should be mailed to Atlanta Regional Loan Center, Attn: COE (262), P.O. Box 100034, Decatur, GA 30031.

Please note that while VA's electronic applications can establish eligibility and issue an online COE in a matter of seconds, not all cases can be processed online. The system can only process those cases for which VA has sufficient data in its records. If a COE cannot be issued immediately, users have the option of submitting an electronic application.

Periods of Eligibility: World War II: (1) active duty service after Sept.15, 1940, and prior to July 26, 1947; (2) discharge under other than dishonorable conditions; and (3) at least 90 days total service unless discharged early for a service-connected disability.

Post-World War II period: (1) active duty service after July 25, 1947, and prior to June 27, 1950; (2) discharge under other than dishonorable conditions; and (3) 181 days continuous active duty service unless discharged early for a service-connected disability.

Korean War: (1) active duty after June 26, 1950, and prior to Feb. 1, 1955; (2) discharge under other than dishonorable conditions; and (3) at least 90 days total service, unless discharged early for a service-connected disability.

Post-Korean War period: (1) active duty after Jan. 31, 1955, and prior to Aug. 5, 1964; (2) discharge under other than dishonorable conditions; (3) 181 days continuous service, unless discharged early for a service-connected disability.

Vietnam War: (1) active duty after Aug. 4, 1964, and prior to May 8, 1975; (2) discharge under other than dishonorable conditions; and (3) 90 days total service, unless discharged early for a service-connected disability. For Veterans who served in the Republic of Vietnam, the beginning date is Feb. 28, 1961.

Post-Vietnam period: (1) active duty after May 7, 1975, and prior to Aug. 2, 1990; (2) active duty for 181 continuous days, all of which occurred after May 7, 1975; and (3) discharge under conditions other than dishonorable or early discharge for service-connected disability.

24-Month Rule: If service was between Sept. 8, 1980, (Oct. 16, 1981, for officers) and Aug. 1, 1990, Veterans must generally complete 24 months of continuous active duty service or the full period (at least 181 days) for which they were called or ordered to active duty, and be discharged under conditions other than dishonorable.

Exceptions are allowed if the Veteran completed at least 181 days of active duty service but was discharged earlier than 24 months for (1) hardship, (2) the convenience of the government, (3) reduction-in-force, (4) certain medical conditions, or (5) service-connected disability.

Gulf War: Veterans of the Gulf War era – Aug. 2, 1990, to a date to be determined – must generally complete 24 months of continuous active duty service or the full period (at least 90 days) for which they were called to active duty, and be discharged under other than dishonorable conditions.

Exceptions are allowed if the Veteran completed at least 90 days of active duty but was discharged earlier than 24 months for (1) hardship, (2) the convenience of the government, (3) reduction-in-force, (4) certain medical conditions, or (5) service-connected disability. Reservists and National Guard members are eligible if they were activated after Aug. 1, 1990, and completed the full period for which they were called to active duty, served at least 90 days, and were discharged under other than dishonorable conditions.

Active Duty Personnel: Until the Gulf War era is ended, persons on active duty are eligible after serving 90 continuous days.

Eligibility for Reserves and/or Guard (not activated): Members of the Reserves and National Guard who are not otherwise eligible for loan guaranty benefits are eligible upon completion of 6 years service in the Reserves or Guard (unless released earlier due to a service-connected disability). The applicant must have received an honorable (a general or under honorable conditions is not qualifying) discharge from such service unless he or she is either in an inactive status awaiting final discharge, or still serving in the Reserves or Guard.

Surviving Spouses: Some spouses of Veterans may have home loan eligibility. They are:

- the unmarried surviving spouse of a Veteran who died as a result of service or service-connected causes
- the surviving spouse of a Veteran who dies on active duty or from service-connected causes, who remarries on or after attaining age 57 and on or after Dec. 16, 2003
- the spouse of an active duty member who is listed as missing in action (MIA) or a prisoner of war (POW) for at least 90 days.

Eligibility under this MIA/POW provision is limited to one-time use only.

Surviving spouses of Veterans who died from non service-connected causes may also be eligible if any of the following conditions are met: The Veteran was rated totally disabled for 10 years or more immediately preceding death, or was rated totally disabled for not less than five years from date of discharge or release from active duty to date of death, or was a former prisoner of war who died after Sept. 30, 1999, and was rated totally disabled for not less than one year immediately preceding death.

Under the Home Loan Guaranty Program, VA does not make loans to Veterans and Servicemembers; VA guarantees loans made by private-sector lenders. The guaranty amount is what VA could pay a lender should the loan go to foreclosure.

VA's guaranteed home loans have no maximum loan amount, only a maximum guaranty amount, which is set in law. However, due to secondary market requirements, lenders typically require that the VA guaranty, plus any downpayment provided by a Veteran, total 25 percent of the loan amount. As a result, an amount equal to four times VA's maximum guaranty amount is customarily referred to as a "loan limit." Loans for the loan limit or less are typically available to Veterans with no downpayment; loans for more than the loan limit generally require downpayments. VA's maximum guaranty amounts are established annually, and vary, depending on the size of the loan and the location of the property.

The following chart lists general information on VA's maximum guaranty. To see the county limits for 2013, select "Loan Limits" on the "Purchase & Cash-Out Refinance Loan" link on http://www.benefits.va.gov/homeloans.

Loan Amount	Maximum Guaranty	Special Provisions
Up to $45,000	50 percent of loan amount	25 percent on Interest Rate Reduction Refinancing Loans
$45,001 - $56,250	$22,500	Same as above
$56,251 - $144,000	40 percent of the loan amount, with a maximum of $36,000	Same as above
$144,000 or more	Up to an amount equal to 25 percent of the county loan limit	Same as above

An eligible borrower can use a VA-guaranteed Interest Rate Reduction Refinancing Loan to refinance an existing VA loan to lower the interest rate and payment. Typically, no credit underwriting is required for this type of loan. The loan may include the entire outstanding balance of the prior loan, the costs of energy-efficient improvements, as well as closing costs, including up to two discount points.

An eligible borrower who wishes to obtain a VA-guaranteed loan to purchase a manufactured home or lot can borrow up to 95 percent of the home's purchase price. The amount VA will guarantee on a manufactured home loan is 40 percent of the loan amount or the Veteran's available entitlement, up to a maximum amount of $20,000. These provisions apply only to a manufactured home that will not be placed on a permanent foundation.

VA Appraisals: No loan can be guaranteed by VA without first being appraised by a VA-assigned fee appraiser. A lender can request a VA appraisal through VA systems. The Veteran borrower typically pays for the appraisal upon completion, according to a fee schedule approved by VA. This VA appraisal estimates the value of the property. It is not an inspection and does not guarantee the house is free of defects. VA guarantees the loan, not the condition of the property. A thorough inspection of the property by a reputable inspection firm may help minimize any problems that could arise after loan closing. In an existing home, particular attention should be given to plumbing, heating, electrical, and roofing components.

Closing Costs: For purchase home loans, payment in cash is required on all closing costs, including title search and recording fees, hazard insurance premiums and prepaid taxes. For refinancing loans, all such costs may be included in the loan, as long as the total loan does not exceed the reasonable value of the property. Interest rate reduction loans may include closing costs, including a maximum of two discount points.

2013 VA Funding Fees: A ffunding fee must be paid to VA unless the Veteran is exempt from such a fee. [See previous discussion in Closing Costs for specific exemptions from the funding fee]. The fee may be paid in cash or included in the loan. Closing costs such as VA appraisal, credit report, loan processing fee, title search, title insurance, recording fees, transfer taxes, survey charges, or hazard insurance may not be included for purchase home loans.

All Veterans, except those who are specified by law as exempt, are charged a VA funding fee (See chart on Page 66). Currently, exemptions from the funding fee are provided for those Veterans and Servicemembers receiving VA disability compensation, those who are rated by VA as eligible to receive compensation as a result of pre-discharge disability examination and rating, and those who would be in receipt of compensation, but who were recalled to active duty or reenlisted and are receiving active-duty pay in lieu of compensation. Additionally, unmarried surviving spouses in receipt of Dependency and Indemnity Compensation are exempt from the funding fee. For all types of loans, the loan amount may include this funding fee.

The VA funding fee and up to $6,000 of energy-efficient improvements can be included in VA loans. However, no other fees, charges, or discount points may be included in the loan amount for regular purchase or construction loans. For refinancing loans, most closing costs may be included in the loan amount.

Required Occupancy: To qualify for a VA home loan, a Veteran or the spouse of an active-duty Servicemember must certify that he or she intends to occupy the home. A dependent child of an active-duty Servicemember also satisfies the occupancy requirement when refinancing a VA-guaranteed loan solely to reduce the interest rate, a Veteran need only certify to prior occupancy.

Financing, Interest Rates and Terms: Veterans obtain VA-guaranteed loans through the usual lending institutions, including banks, credit unions, and mortgage brokers. VA-guaranteed loans can have either a fixed interest rate or an adjustable rate, where the interest rate may adjust up to one percent annually and up to five percent over the life of the loan. VA does not set the interest rate. Interest rates are negotiable between the lender and borrower on all loan types.

Veterans may also choose a different type of adjustable rate mortgage called a hybrid ARM, where the initial interest rate remains fixed for three to 10 years. If the rate remains fixed for less than five years, the rate adjustment cannot be more than one percent annually and five percent over the life of the loan. For a hybrid ARM with an initial fixed period of five years or more, the initial adjustment may be up to two percent. The Secretary has the authority to determine annual adjustments thereafter. Currently annual adjustments may be up to two percentage points and six percent over the life of the loan.

If the lender charges discount points on the loan, the Veteran may negotiate with the seller as to who will pay points or if they will be split between buyer and seller. Points paid by the Veteran may not be included in the loan (with the exception that up to two points may be included in interest rate reduction refinancing loans). The term of the loan may be for as long as 30 years and 32 days.

Loan Assumption Requirements and Liability: VA loans made on or after March 1, 1988, are not assumable without the prior approval of VA or its authorized agent (usually the lender collecting the monthly payments). To approve the assumption, the lender must ensure that the borrower is a satisfactory credit risk and will assume all of the Veteran's liabilities on the loan. If approved, the borrower will have to pay a funding fee that the lender sends to VA, and the Veteran will be released from liability to the federal government. A release of liability does not mean that a Veteran's guaranty entitlement is restored. That occurs only if the borrower is an eligible Veteran who agrees to substitute his or her entitlement for that of the seller. If a Veteran allows assumption of a loan without prior approval, then the lender may demand immediate and full payment of the loan, and the Veteran may be liable if the loan is foreclosed and VA has to pay a claim under the loan guaranty.

Loans made prior to March 1, 1988, are generally freely assumable, but Veterans should still request VA's approval in order to be released of liability. Veterans whose loans were closed after Dec. 31, 1989, usually have no liability to the government following a foreclosure, except in cases involving fraud, misrepresentation, or bad faith, such as allowing an unapproved assumption. However, for the entitlement to be restored, any loss suffered by VA must be paid in full.

2013 VA Funding Fee Rates

Loan Category	Active Duty and Veterans	Reservists and National Guard
Loans for purchase or construction with downpayments of less than 5 percent, refinancing, and home improvement	2.15 percent	2.40 percent
Loans for purchase or construction with downpayments of at least 5 percent but less than 10 percent	1.50 percent	1.75 percent
Loans for purchase or construction with downpayments of 10percent or more	1.25 percent	1.50 percent
Loans for manufactured homes	1 percent	1 percent
Interest rate reduction refinancing loans	.50 percent	.50 percent
Assumption of a VA-guaranteed loan	.50 percent	.50 percent
Second or subsequent use of entitlement with no downpayment	3.3 percent	3.3 percent

VA Assistance to Veterans in Default: VA urges all Veterans who are encountering problems making their mortgage payments to speak with their servicers as soon as possible to explore options to avoid foreclosure. Contrary to popular opinion, servicers do not want to foreclose because foreclosure costs a lot of money. Depending on a Veteran's specific situation, servicers may offer any of the following options to avoid foreclosure:

- Repayment Plan – The borrower makes regular installment each month plus part of the missed installments.
- Special Forbearance – The servicer agrees not to initiate fore closure to allow time for borrowers to repay the missed installments. An example of when this would be likely is when a borrower is waiting for a tax refund.
- Loan Modification - Provides the borrower a fresh start by adding the delinquency to the loan balance and establishing a new payment schedule.
- Additional time to arrange a private sale – The servicer agrees to delay foreclosure to allow a sale to close if the loan will be paid off.
- Short Sale – When the servicer agrees to allow a borrower to sell his/her home for a lesser amount than what is currently required to payoff the loan.
- Deed-in-Lieu of Foreclosure - The borrower voluntarily agrees to deed the property to the servicer instead of going through a lengthy foreclosure process.

Servicemembers Civil Relief Act
Veteran borrowers may be able to request relief pursuant to the Servicemembers Civil Relief Act (SCRA). In order to qualify for certain protections available under the Act, their obligation must have originated prior to their current period of active military service. SCRA may provide a lower interest rate during military service and for up to one year after service ends, and provide forbearance, or prevent foreclosure or eviction up to nine months from period of military service.

Assistance to Veterans with VA-Guaranteed Home Loans
When a VA-guaranteed home loan becomes delinquent, VA may provide supplemental servicing assistance to help cure the default. The servicer has the primary responsibility of servicing the loan to resolve the default.

However, in cases where the servicer is unable to help the Veteran borrower, VA has loan technicians in eight Regional Loan Centers and two special servicing centers who take an active role in interceding with the mortgage servicer to explore all options to avoid foreclosure. Veterans with VA-guaranteed home loans can call 1-877 827-3702 to reach the nearest VA office where loan specialists are prepared to discuss potential ways to help save the loan.

VA Acquired Property Foreclosures
VA acquires properties as a result of foreclosures VA-guaranteed and VA-owned loans. A private contractor is currently marketing the acquired properties through listing agents using local Multiple Listing Services. A listing of "VA Properties for Sale" may be found at http:// listings.vrmco.com/. Contact a real estate agent for information on purchasing a VA-acquired property.

Preventing Veteran Homelessness
Veterans who feel they may be facing homelessness as a result of losing their home can call 1-877-4AID VET (877-424-3838) or go to http://www.va.gov/HOMELESS/index.asp to receive assistance from VA.

Assistance to Veterans with Non-VA Guaranteed Home Loans
For Veterans or Servicemembers who have a conventional or subprime loan, VA has a network of eight Regional Loan Centers and two special servicing centers that can offer advice and guidance. Borrowers may visit www.benefits.va.gov/homeloans/, or call toll free -1-877-827-3702 to speak with a VA loan technician. However, unlike when a Veteran has a VA-guaranteed home loan, VA does not have the legal authority to intervene on the borrower's behalf. It is imperative that a borrower contact his/her servicer as quickly as possible.

VA Refinancing of a Non-VA Guaranteed Home Loan
Veterans with conventional home loans now have new options for refinancing to a VA-guaranteed home loan. These new options are available as a result of the Veterans' Benefits Improvement Act of 2008. Veterans who wish to refinance their subprime or conventional mortgage may now do so for up t o 100 percent of the value of the property, which is up from the previous limit of 90 percent.

Additionally, Congress raised VA's maximum loan guaranty for these types of refinancing loans. Loan limits were effectively raised from $144,000 to $417,000. High-cost counties have even higher maximum loan limits. VA county loan limits can be found at http://www. benefits.va.gov/homeloans/. These changes will allow more qualified Veterans to refinance through VA, allowing for savings on interest costs and avoiding foreclosure.

Other Assistance for Delinquent Veteran Borrowers

If VA is not able to help a Veteran borrower retain his/her home (whether a VA-guaranteed loan or not), the HOPE NOW Alliance may be of assistance. HOPE NOW is a joint alliance consisting of servicers, counselors, and investors whose main goal is to assist distressed borrowers retain their homes and avoid foreclosure. They have expertise in financial counseling, as well as programs that take advantage of relief measures that VA cannot. HOPE NOW provides outreach, counseling and assistance to homeowners who have the willingness and ability to keep their homes but are facing financial difficulty as a result of the crisis in the mortgage market. The HOPE NOW Alliance can be reached at (888) 995-HOPE (4673), or by visiting www.hopenow.com.

For more information go to http://www.benefits.va.gov/homeloans/, or call (877) 827-3702

Loans for Native American Veterans

Eligible Native American Veterans can obtain a loan from VA to purchase, construct, or improve a home on Federal Trust Land, or to reduce the interest rate on such a VA loan. Native American Direct Loans are only available if a memorandum of understanding exists between the tribal organization and VA.

Veterans who are not Native American, but who are married to Native American non-Veterans, may be eligible for a direct loan under this program. To be eligible for such a loan, the qualified non-Native American Veteran and the Native American spouse must reside on Federal Trust Land, and both the Veteran and spouse must have a meaningful interest in the dwelling or lot.

The following safeguards have been established to protect Veterans:

1. VA may suspend from the loan program those who take unfair advantage of Veterans or discriminate because of race, color, religion, sex, disability, family status, or national origin.
2. The builder of a new home (or manufactured) is required to give the purchasing Veteran either a one-year warranty or a 10-year insurance-backed protection plan.
3. The borrower obtaining a loan may only be charged closing

costs allowed by VA.
4. The borrower can prepay without penalty the entire loan or any part not less than one installment or $100.
5. VA encourages holders to extend forbearance if a borrower becomes temporarily
unable to meet the terms of the loan.

Chapter 7

VA Life Insurance

For complete details on government life insurance, visit the VA Internet site at www.insurance.va.gov/ or call VA's Insurance Center toll-free at 1-800-669-8477. Specialists are available between the hours of 8:30 a.m. and 6 p.m., Eastern Time, to discuss premium payments, insurance dividends, address changes, policy loans, naming beneficiaries and reporting the death of the insured.

If the insurance policy number is not known, send whatever information is available, such as the Veteran's VA file number, date of birth, Social Security number, military serial number or military service branch and dates of service to:

Department of Veterans Affairs
Insurance Center
PO Box 42954
Philadelphia, PA 19101

For information about Servicemembers' Group Life Insurance, Veterans Group Life Insurance, Servicemembers' Group Life Insurance Traumatic Injury Protection, or Servicemembers' Group Life Insurance Family Coverage, visit the Website above or call the Office of Servicemembers' Group Life Insurance directly at 1-800-419-1473.

Servicemembers' Group Life Insurance: The following are automatically insured for $400,000 under Servicemembers' Group Life Insurance (SGLI)
　　1. Active-duty members of the Army, Navy, Air Force, Marines and Coast Guard.
　　2. Commissioned members of the National Oceanic and Atmospheric Administration (NOAA) and the Public Health Service (PHS).
　　3. Cadets or midshipmen of the U.S. military academies.
　　4. Members, cadets and midshipmen of the ROTC while engaged in authorized training and practice cruises.
　　5. Members of the Ready Reserves/National Guard who are

scheduled to perform at least 12 periods of inactive training
per year.
6. Members who volunteer for a mobilization category in the
Individual Ready Reserve.

Individuals may elect in writing to be covered for a lesser amount or
no coverage. SGLI coverage is available in $50,000 increments up to
the maximum of $400,000.

Full-time Servicemembers on active duty are covered 365 days per
year. Coverage is in effect during the period of active duty or inactive duty training and for 120 days following separation or release
from duty. Reservists or National Guard members who have been
assigned to a unit in which they are scheduled to perform at least 12
periods of inactive duty that is creditable for retirement purposes are
also covered 365 days of the year and for 120 days following separation or release from duty.

Part-time coverage is provided for Reservists or National Guard
members who do not qualify for the full-time coverage described
above. Part-time coverage generally applies to Reservists/National
Guard members who drill only a few days in a year. These individuals are covered only while on active duty or active duty for training,
or traveling to and from such duty. Members covered part-time do
not receive 120 days of free coverage after separation unless they
incur or aggravate a disability during a period of duty

SGLI Traumatic Injury Protection: Members of the armed services
serve our nation heroically during times of great need, but what hap-
pens when they experience great needs of their own because they
have sustained a traumatic injury? Servicemembers' Group Life
Insurance Traumatic Injury Protection (TSGLI) helps severely injured
Servicemembers who have suffered physical losses through their
time of need with a one-time payment. The amount varies depending on the loss, but it could make a difference in the lives of Servicemembers by allowing their families to be with them during their
recovery. TSGLI helps them with unforeseen expenses or gives them
a financial head start on life after recovery.

TSGLI is attached to Servicemembers' Group Life Insurance (SGLI).
An additional $1.00 is added to the Servicemember's SGLI premium

to cover TSGLI. After December 1, 2005, all Servicemembers who are covered by SGLI are automatically also covered by TSGLI. TSGLI cannot be declined unless the Servicemember also declines basic SGLI. TSGLI claims are adjudicated by the individual military branches of service.

In addition, there is retroactive TSGLI coverage for Servicemembers who sustained a qualifying loss between Oct. 7, 2001 and November 30, 2005, regardless of where it occurred . TSGLI coverage is payable to these Servicemembers regardless of whether they had SGLI coverage in force.

For more information, and branch of service contact information, visit www.insurance.va.gov/sgliSite/TSGLI/TSGLI.htm, or call 1-800-237-1336 (Army); 1-800-368-3202 (Navy); 1-877-216-0825 (Marine Corps); 1-800-433-0048 (Active Duty Air Force); 1-800-525-0102 (Air Force Reserves); 1-240-612-9072 (Air National Guard); 1-703-872-6647- (U.S. Coast Guard); 1-301-427-3280 (PHS); or 1-301-713-3444 (NOAA).

Servicemembers' Group Life Insurance Family Coverage: FSGLI Family Coverage consists of spousal coverage and dependent child coverage. FSGLI provides up to $100,000 of life insurance coverage for spouses of Servicemembers with full-time SGLI coverage, not to exceed the amount of SGLI the member has in force. FSGLI is a Servicemembers' benefit; the member pays the premium and is the only person allowed to be the beneficiary of the coverage. FSGLI spousal coverage ends when: 1) the Servicemember elects in writing to terminate coverage on the spouse; 2) the Servicemember elects to terminate his or her own SGLI coverage; 3) the Servicemember dies; 4) the Servicemember separates from service; or 5) the Servicemember is divorced from the spouse. The insured spouse may convert his or her FSGLI coverage to a permanent policy offered by participating private insurers within 120 days of the date of any of the termination events noted above. FSGLI dependent coverage of $10,000 is also automatically provided for dependent children of Servicemembers insured under SGLI, with no premium required.

Veterans' Group Life Insurance: SGLI may be converted to Veterans' Group Life Insurance (VGLI), which provides renewable term coverage to:
   1. Veterans who had full-time SGLI coverage upon speration

from active duty or the reserves.
2. Members of the Ready Reserves/National Guard with part-time SGLI coverage who incur a disability or aggravate a pre-existing disability during a period of active duty or a period of inactive duty for less than 31 days that renders them uninsurable at standard premium rates.
3. Members of the Individual Ready Reserve and Inactive National Guard.

Servicemembers must apply for VGLI within one year and 120 days from separation . Servicemembers discharged on or after November 1, 2012 who apply for VGLI within 240 days of separation do not need to submit evidence of good health, while Servicemembers who apply after the 240-day period must submit evidence of insurability..

Effective April 11, 2011, VGLI insureds who are under age 60 and have less than $400,000 in coverage can purchase up to $25,000 of additional coverage on each five-year anniversary of their coverage, up to the maximum $400,000. No medical underwriting is required for the additional coverage.

SGLI Disability Extension: Servicemembers who are totally disabled at the time of separation (unable to work), can apply for the SGLI Disability Extension, which provides free coverage for up to two years from the date of separation. To apply, Servicmembers must complete and return SGLV 8715, the SGLI Disability Extension Application.

Those covered under the SGLI Disability Extension are automatically converted to VGLI at the end of their extension period, subject to the payment of premiums. VGLI is convertible at any time to a permanent plan policy with any participating commercial insurance company.

Accelerated Death Benefits: Like many private life insurance companies, the SGLI, FSGLI and VGLI programs offer an accelerated benefits option to terminally ill insureds. An insured member is considered to be terminally ill if he or she has a written medical prognosis of 9 months or less to live. All terminally ill members are eligible to receive up to 50 percent of their SGLI or VGLI coverage in a lump sum. Accelerated benefits paid prior to death are not, of course, available for payment to survivors. To apply, an insured

member must submit SGLV 8284, Servicemember/Veteran Accelerated Benefit Option Form.

Service-Disabled Veterans' Insurance: Veterans who separated
from Service on or after April 25, 1951 under other than dishonorable
conditions who have service-connected disabilities, even zero percent, disability but are otherwise in good health, may apply to VA for
up to $10,000 in life insurance coverage under the Service-Disabled
Veterans' Insurance (S-DVI) program. Applications must be submitted within two years from the date of being notified of the approval of
a new service-connected disability by VA. .
Veterans who are totally disabled may apply for a waiver of premiums and additional supplemental insurance coverage of up to
$30,000. However, premiums cannot be waived on the additional
supplemental insurance. To be eligible for this type of supplemental
insurance, Veterans must meet all of the following three requirements:
1. Be under age 65.
2. Be eligible for a waiver of premiums due to total disability.
3. Apply for additional insurance within one year from the date of
   notification of waiver approval on the basic S-DVI policy.

Veterans' Mortgage Life Insurance: VMLI is mortgage protection
insurance available to severely disabled Veterans who have been
approved by VA for a Specially Adapted Housing Grant (SAH). Maximum coverage is the smaller of the existing mortgage balance or
$200,000, and is payable only to the mortgage company. Protection
is issued automatically following SAH approval, provided the Veteran
submits mortgage information required to establish a premium and
does not decline coverage. Coverage automatically terminates when
the mortgage is paid off. If a mortgage is disposed of through sale
of the property, VMLI may be obtained on the mortgage of another
home.

Other Insurance Information
The following information applies to policies issued to World War
II, Korean, and Vietnam-era Veterans and any Service-Disabled
Veterans Insurance policies. Policies in this group are prefixed by the
letters K, V, RS, W, J, JR, JS, or RH.

Insurance Dividends Issued Annually: World War II, and Korean-era Veterans with active policies beginning with the letters V, RS, W, J, JR, JS, or K earn tax-free dividends annually on the policy anniversary date. (Policies prefixed by RH do not earn dividends.) Policyholders do not need to apply for dividends, but may select from among the following dividend options:

1. Cash: The dividend is paid directly to the insured either by a mailed check or by direct deposit to a bank account.
2. Paid-Up Additional Insurance: The dividend is used to purchase additional insurance coverage.
3. Credit or Deposit: The dividend is held in an account for the policyholder with interest. Withdrawals from the account can be made at any time. The interest rate may be adjusted.
4. Net Premium Billing Options: These options use the dividend to pay the annual policy premium. If the dividend exceeds the premium, the policyholder has options to choose how the remainder is used. If the dividend is not enough to pay an annual premium, the policyholder is billed the balance.
5. Other Dividend Options: Dividends can also be used to repay a loan or pay premiums in advance.

Reinstating Lapsed Insurance: Lapsed term policies may be reinstated within five years from the date of lapse. A five-year term policy that is not lapsed at the end of the term is automatically renewed for an additional five years. Lapsed permanent plans may be reinstated within certain time limits and with certain health requirements. Reinstated permanent plan policies require repayment of all back premiums, plus interest.

Converting Term Policies: Term policies are renewed automatically every five years, with premiums increasing at each renewal. Premiums do not increase after age 70. Term policies may be converted to permanent plans, which have fixed premiums for life and earn cash and loan values.

Dividends on Capped Term Policies: Effective Sept. 2000, VA provides either a cash dividend or paid-up insurance on term policies whose premiums have been capped. Veterans with National Service Life Insurance (NSLI) term insurance that has renewed at age 71 or older and who stop paying premiums on their policies will be given a "termination dividend." This dividend can either be received as a cash payment or used to purchase a reduced amount of paid-up insurance, which insures the Veteran for life with no premium payments required. The amount of the reduced paid-up insurance remains level. This does not apply to S-DVI (RH) policies.

Borrowing on Policies: Policyholders with permanent plan policies may borrow up to 94 percent of the cash surrender value of their insurance after the insurance is in force for one year or more. Interest is compounded annually. The loan interest rate is variable and may be obtained by calling toll-free 1-800-669-8477.

Chapter 8

Burial and Memorial Benefits

Veterans discharged from active duty under conditions other than dishonorable; Servicemembers who die while on active duty, active duty for training, or inactive duty training; and spouses and dependent children of Veterans and active duty service members, may be eligible for VA burial and memorial benefits. (For the purposes of this chapter, the term "Veteran" includes eligible persons who die during active duty service.) The Veteran does not have to die before a spouse or dependent child can be eligible for burial or memorial benefits.

Burial in VA National Cemeteries

Burial in a VA national cemetery is available for eligible Veterans, spouses and dependents at no cost and includes the gravesite, grave-liner, opening and closing of the grave, a headstone or marker, and perpetual care as part of a national shrine. For Veterans, benefits may also include a burial flag (with case for active duty), and military funeral honors.

With certain exceptions, active duty service beginning after Sept. 7, 1980, as an enlisted person, and after Oct. 16, 1981, as an officer, must be for a minimum of 24 consecutive months or the full period of active duty (as in the case of reservists or National Guard members called to active duty for a limited duration). Active duty for training, by itself, while serving in the reserves or National Guard, is not sufficient to confer eligibility. Reservists and National Guard members, as well as their spouses and dependent children, are eligible if they were entitled to retired pay at the time of death, or would have been upon reaching requisite age. See Chapter 8 for more information.

Certain otherwise eligible individuals found to have committed federal or state capital crimes are barred from burial or memorialization in a VA national cemetery, and from receipt of Government-furnished headstones, markers, medallions, burial flags, and Presidential Memorial Certificates. Veterans and other claimants for VA burial benefits have the right to appeal decisions made by VA regarding eligibility for national cemetery burial or other memorial benefits. Chapter 13 discusses the procedures for appealing VA claims. This chapter contains information on the full range of VA burial and memorial benefits. Readers with questions may contact the nearest national cemetery, listed by state in the VA Facilities section of this book, call 1-800-827-1000, or visit the web site at www.cem.va.gov/.

Surviving spouses of Veterans who died on or after Jan. 1, 2000, do not lose eligibility for burial in a national cemetery if they remarry. Unmarried dependent children of Veterans who are under 21 years of age, or under 23 years of age if a full-time student at an approved educational institution, are eligible for burial. Unmarried adult children who become physically or mentally disabled and incapable of self-support before age 21, or age 23 if a full-time student, also are eligible.

Certain Parents of servicemembers who die as a result of hostile activity or from combat training-related injuries may be eligible for burial in a national cemetery with their child. The biological or adopted parents of a servicemember who died in combat or while performing training in preparation for a combat mission, who leaves no surviving spouse or dependent child, may be buried with the deceased servicemember if there is available space. Eligibility is limited to servicemembers who died on or after Oct. 7, 2001, and biological or adoptive parents who died on or after Oct. 13, 2010.

The next of kin or authorized representative (e.g., funeral director) makes interment arrangements at time of need by contacting the National Cemetery Scheduling Office (see information available at http://www.cem.va.gov/bbene/need.asp) or, in some cases, the national cemetery in which burial is desired. VA normally does not conduct burials on weekends. Gravesites cannot be reserved; however, VA will honor reservations made before 1973 by the Department of the Army.

VA's National Cemetery Scheduling Office or local national cemetery directors verify eligibility for burial. A copy of the Veteran's discharge document that specifies the period(s) of active duty and character of service is usually sufficient to determine eligibility. A copy of the deceased's death certificate and proof of relationship to the Veteran (for eligible family members) may be required.

VA operates 131 national cemeteries, of which 72 are currently open for both new casket and cremation interments and 18 may accept new interment of cremated remains only. Burial options are limited to those available at a specific cemetery and may include in-ground casket, or interment of cremated remains in a columbarium, in-ground, or in a scattering area. Contact the national cemetery directly, or visit our website at http://www.cem.va.gov to determine if a particular cemetery is open for new burials, and what other options are available.

Headstones, Markers and Medallions

Veterans, Veterans, active duty service members, and retired Reservists and National Guard service members, are eligible for an inscribed headstone or marker for their unmarked grave at any cemetery – national, state veterans, tribal, or private. VA will deliver a headstone or marker at no cost, anywhere in the world.

For eligible Veterans or service members buried in a private ceme-tery whose deaths occurred on or after Nov. 1, 1990, VA may furnish a government headstone or marker (even if the grave is already marked with a private one); or VA may furnish a medallion to affix to an already existing privately-purchased headstone or marker.

Spouses and dependent children are eligible for a government head-stone or marker only if they are buried in a national or State Veterans cemetery.

Flat markers are available in bronze, granite or marble. Upright headstones come in granite or marble. The style provided will be consistent with existing monuments at the place of burial. Niche markers are available to mark columbaria used for inurnment of cremated remains. Medallions are made of bronze and are available in three sizes: 5-inch, 3-inch, and 1 ½-inches. Headstones, mark-ers and medallions previously furnished by the government may be replaced at the government's expense if badly deteriorated, illegible, vandalized or stolen.

Headstones or markers for VA national cemeteries will be ordered by the cemetery director using information provided by the next of kin or authorized representative.

Headstones or Markers for private cemeteries: Before ordering, the next of kin or authorized representative should check with the cemetery to ensure that the Government-furnished headstone or marker will be accepted. All installation fees at private cemeteries are the responsibility of the applicant. To submit a claim for a headstone or marker for a gravesite in a private cemetery, use VA Form 40-1330, Application for Standard Government Headstone or Marker (available at http://www.va.gov/vaforms/). A copy of the Veteran's military discharge document is required. Mail forms to Memorial Programs Service, Department of Veterans Affairs, 5109 Russell Road, Quantico, VA 22134-3903. The form and supporting documents may also be faxed toll free to 1-800-455-7143.

"In Memory Of" Markers: VA provides memorial headstones and markers with "In Memory Of" as the first line of inscription for those whose remains have not been recovered or identified, were buried at sea, donated to science or cremated and scattered. Eligibility is the same as for regular headstones and markers. There is no fee when the "In Memory Of" marker is placed in a national cemetery. All installation fees at private cemeteries are the responsibility of the applicant. Memorial headstones/markers for spouses and dependents can be provided only for placement in a national or State veterans cemetery.

Inscriptions: Headstones and markers must be inscribed with the name of the deceased, branch of service, and year of birth and death. They also may be inscribed with other optional information, including an emblem of belief and, space permitting, additional text including military rank; war service such as "World War II;" complete dates of birth and death; military awards; military organizations; civilian or Veteran affiliations; and personalized words of endearment.

Medallion in lieu of government headstone or marker for private cemeteries: For Veterans or service members whose death occurred on or after Nov. 1, 1990, VA is authorized to provide a medallion instead of a headstone or marker if the grave is in a private cemetery and already marked with a privately-purchased headstone or marker. To submit a claim for a medallion to be affixed to a private headstone/marker in a private cemetery, use VA Form 40-1330M, Claim for Government Medallion (available at http://www.va.gov/vaforms). A copy of the Veteran's military discharge document is required. Mail forms to Memorial Programs Service, Department of Veterans Affairs, 5109 Russell Road, Quantico, VA 22134-3903. The form and supporting documents may also be faxed toll free to 1-800-

455-7143.

To check the status of a claim for a headstone or marker for placement in a national, state, or tribal Veterans cemetery, please call
the cemetery. To check the status of one being placed in a private
cemetery, please contact the Applicant Assistance Unit at 1-800-697-
6947 or via email at mps.headstone@va.gov.

Other Memorialization

Presidential Memorial Certificates are issued to recognize the
military service of honorably discharged deceased Veterans and persons who died in the active military, naval, or air service. Next of kin,
relatives and other loved ones may apply for a certificate by mailing,
or faxing a completed and signed VA Form 40-0247, Presidential
Memorial Certificate Request Form (available at http://www.va.gov/
vaforms/), along with a copy of the Veteran's military discharge
documents or proof of honorable military service. The processing of
requests sent without supporting documents will be delayed until eligibility can determined. Eligibility requirements can be found at www.
cem.va.gov.

Burial Flags: Generally, VA will furnish a U.S. burial flag to memorialize Veterans who received an other than dishonorable discharge.
This includes certain persons who served in the organized military
forces of the Commonwealth of the Philippines while in service of
the U.S armed forces and who died on or after April 25, 1951. Also
eligible for a burial flag are Veterans who were entitled to retired pay
for service in the Reserve or National Guard, or would have been
entitled if over age 60; and members or former members of the Selected Reserve who served their initial obligation, or were discharged
for a disability incurred or aggravated in the line of duty, or died while
a member of the Selected Reserve. The next of kin may apply for the
flag at any VA regional office or U.S. Post Office by completing VA
Form 21-2008, Application for United States Flag for Burial Purposes
(available at http://www.va.gov/vaforms/). In most cases, a funeral
director will help the family obtain the flag.

Reimbursement of Burial Expenses: VA will pay a burial allowance
up to $2,000 if the Veteran's death is service-connected. In such
cases, the person who bore the Veteran's burial expenses may claim
reimbursement from VA.

In some cases, VA will pay the cost of transporting the remains of a Veteran whose death was service-connected to the nearest national cemetery with available gravesites. There is no time limit for filing reimbursement claims in service-connected death cases.

Burial Allowance: VA will pay a burial and funeral allowance of up to $2,000 for Veterans who die from service-connected causes. VA will pay a burial and funeral allowance of up to $300 for Veterans who, at the time of death from nonservice-connected causes, were entitled to receive pension or compensation or would have been entitled if they were not receiving military retirement pay. VA will pay a burial and funeral allowance of up to $722 when the Veteran's death occurs in a VA facility, a VA-contracted nursing home or a state Veterans nursing home. In cases in which the Veteran's death was not service con- nected, claims must be filed within two years after burial or crema- tion.

Plot Allowance: VA will pay a plot allowance of up to $722 when a Veteran is buried in a cemetery not under U.S. government ju- risdiction if: the Veteran was discharged from active duty because of disability incurred or aggravated in the line of duty; the Veteran was receiving compensation or pension or would have been if the Veteran was not receiving military retired pay; or the Veteran died in a VA facility. The plot allowance may be paid to the state for the cost of a plot or interment in a state-owned cemetery reserved solely for Veteran burials if the Veteran is buried without charge. Burial expenses paid by the deceased's employer or a state agency will not be reimbursed.

Military Funeral Honors: Upon request, DoD will provide military funeral honors consisting of folding and the presenting of the United States flag and the playing of "Taps." A funeral honors detail consists of two or more uniformed members of the armed forces, with at least one member from the deceased's branch of service.

Family members should inform their funeral director if they want military funeral honors. DoD maintains a toll-free number (1-877-MIL- HONR) for use by funeral directors only to request honors. VA can help arrange honors for burials at VA national cemeteries. Veterans service organizations or volunteer groups may help provide honors. For more information, visit www.militaryfuneralhonors.osd.mil/.

Veterans Cemeteries Administered by Other Agencies

Department of the Army: Administers Arlington National Cemetery and other Army installation cemeteries. Eligibility is generally more restrictive than at VA national cemeteries. For information, call (703) 607-8000, write Superintendent, Arlington National Cemetery, Arlington, VA 22211, or visit www.arlingtoncemetery.mil/.

Department of the Interior: Administers two active national cemeteries – Andersonville National Cemetery in Georgia and Andrew Johnson National Cemetery in Tennessee. Eligibility is similar to VA national cemeteries. For information, call (202) 208-4747, write Department of Interior, National Park Service 1849 C. St. NW, Washington, D.C. 20240.

State and Tribal Veterans Cemeteries: Currently 87 state and four Tribal Veterans cemeteries offer burial options for Veterans and their families. These cemeteries have similar eligibility requirements and some require state residency. Some services, particularly for family members, may require a fee. Contact the state or tribal veterans cemetery or the state veterans affairs office for information. To locate a State or Tribal Veterans cemetery, visit www.cem.va.gov/cem/scg/lsvc.asp.

Chapter 9
Reserve and National Guard

Eligibility for VA Benefits

Reservists who serve on active duty establish Veteran status and may be eligible for the full range of VA benefits, depending on the length of active military service and a discharge or release from active duty under conditions other than dishonorable. In addition, Reservists not activated may qualify for some VA benefits.

National Guard members can establish eligibility for VA benefits if activated for federal service during a period of war or domestic emergency. Activation for other than federal service does not qualify National Guard members for all VA benefits. Claims for VA benefits based on federal service filed by members of the National Guard should include a copy of the military orders, presidential proclamation, or executive order that clearly demonstrates the federal nature of the service.

Qualifying for VA Health Care

Under the "Combat Veteran" authority, Combat Veterans who were discharged or released from active service on or after Jan. 28, 2003, are eligible for enrollment in Priority Group 6, unless eligible for enrollment in a higher priority group. This authority provides a 5-year enrollment period, which begins on the discharge or separation date. These Combat Veterans are eligible for health care services and community living care for conditions possibly related to their military service, and are not required to disclose their income information unless they would like to be considered for a higher priority status, beneficiary travel benefits, or exemption of co-pays for care unrelated to their military service.

Activated Reservists and members of the National Guard are eligible if they served on active duty in a theater of combat operations after Nov. 11, 1998, and were discharged under other than dishonorable conditions.

Veterans who enroll with VA under this authority will continue to be enrolled even after their enhanced eligibility period ends. At the end of their enhanced eligibility period, Veterans enrolled in Priority Group 6 may be shifted to a lower priority group depending on their income level. For additional information, call 1-877-222-VETS (8387).

OEF/OIF/OND Veterans may be eligible for a one-time dental evaluation and treatment following separation from service, if they did not have a dental exam prior to separation. Veterans must request a dental appointment within the first 180 days post separation from active duty.

Disability Benefits

VA pays monthly compensation benefits for disabilities incurred or aggravated during active duty, or active duty for training as a result of injury or disease, or inactive duty training for disabilities due to injury, heart attack, or stroke. Additionally, the discharge must be under other than dishonorable conditions. For additional information see Chapter 2, "Service-connected Disabilities."

Montgomery GI Bill – Selected Reserve

Members of reserve elements of the Army, Navy, Air Force, Marine Corps and Coast Guard, and members of the Army National Guard and the Air National Guard, may be entitled to up to 36 months of educational benefits under the Montgomery GI Bill (MGIB) – Selected Reserve. To be eligible, the participant must:
1. Have a six-year obligation in the Selected Reserve or National Guard signed after June 30, 1985, or, if an officer, agree to serve six years in addition to the original obligation.
2. Complete initial active duty for training (IADT).
3. Meet the requirement to receive a high school diploma or equivalency certificate before Completing IADT..
4. Remain in good standing in a Selected Reserve or National Guard unit.

Reserve components determine eligibility for benefits. VA does not make decisions about eligibility and cannot make payments until the Reserve component has determined eligibility and notified VA.

Period of Eligibility: Benefits generally end the day a reservist or National Guard member separates from the military. Additionally, if in the Selected Reserve and called to active duty, VA can generally extend the eligibility period by the length of time on active duty plus four months for each period of active duty. Once this extension is granted, it will not be taken awayafter leaving the Selected Reserve.

Eligible members separated because of unit deactivation, a dis-ability that was not caused by misconduct, or otherwise involuntarily separated during Oct. 1, 1991, through December 31, 2001, have 14 years after their eligibility date to use benefits. Similarly, members involuntarily separated from the Selected Reserve due to a deacti-vation of their unit between Oct. 1, 2007, and Sept. 30, 2014, may receive a 14-year period of eligibility.

Payments: The rate for full-time training effective Oct. 1, 2012, is $356 a month for 36 months. Part-time benefits are reduced propor-tionately. For complete current rates, visit www.gibill.va.gov. DoD may make additional contributions.

Training: Participants may pursue training at a college or university, or take technical training at any approved facility. Training includes undergraduate, graduate, or post-graduate courses; state licensure and certification; courses for a certificate or diploma from business, technical or vocational schools; cooperative training; apprenticeship or on-the-job training; correspondence courses; independent study programs; flight training; entrepreneurship training; remedial, defi-ciency or refresher courses needed to complete a program of study; or preparatory courses for tests required or used for admission to an institution of higher learning or graduate school.
Accelerated payments for certain high-cost programs are authorized effective Jan. 28, 2008

Work-Study: See page 55

Educational and Vocational Counseling: Refer to Chapter 10, "Transition Assistance", for detailed information on available ser-vices.

Reserve Educational Assistance Program (REAP)
This program provides educational assistance to members of Na-tional Guard and Reserve components who are called or ordered to active duty service in response to a war or national emergency as declared by the President or Congress. Visit www.gibill.va.gov for more information.

Eligibility: Eligibility is determined by DoD or the Department of Homeland Security. Generally, a Servicemember who serves on active duty on or after Sept. 11, 2001, for at least 90 consecutive days, or accumulates a total of three or more of years of service is eligible.

Payments: Reserve or National Guard members whose eligibility is based upon continuous service receive a payment rate based upon their number of continuous days on active duty. Members who qualify after the accumulation of three or more years of aggregate active duty service receive the full payment allowable.

Reserve Educational Assistance Rates

Active Duty Service	Monthly Payment Rate for Full-Time Students
90 days but less than one year	$625.60
One year but less than two years	$938.40
Two or more continuous years	$1,251.20

Training: Participants may pursue training at a college or university, or take technical training at any approved facility. Training includes undergraduate, graduate, or post-graduate courses; state licensure and certification courses; courses for a certificate or diploma from business, technical or vocational schools; cooperative training; apprenticeship or on-the-job training; correspondence courses; independent study programs; flight training; entrepreneurship training; remedial, deficiency, or refresher courses needed to complete a program of study; or preparatory courses for tests required or used for admission to an institution of higher learning or graduate school. Accelerated payments for certain high-cost programs are authorized.

Period of Eligibility: Prior to Jan. 28, 2008, members of the Selected Reserve called to active duty were eligible as long as they continued to serve in the Selected Reserve. They lost eligibility if they went into the Inactive Ready Reserve (IRR). Members of the IRR called to active duty were eligible as long as they stayed in the IRR or Selected Reserve.

Effective Jan. 28, 2008, members who are called up from the Selected Reserve, complete their REAP-qualifying period of active duty service, and then return to the Selected Reserve for the remainder of their service contract, have 10 years to use their benefits after separation.

In addition, members who are called up from the IRR or Inactive National Guard (ING), complete their REAP-qualifying period of active duty service, and then enter the Selected Reserve to complete their service contract, have 10 years to use their benefits after separation.

Work-Study Program: See page 55.

Educational and Vocational Counseling: Refer to Chapter 10, "Transition Assistance", for detailed information on available services.

Home Loan Guaranty

National Guard members and reservists are eligible for a VA home loan if they have completed at least six years of honorable service, are mobilized for active duty service for a period of at least 90 days, or are discharged because of a service-connected disability.

Reservists who do not qualify for VA housing loan benefits may be eligible for loans on favorable terms insured by the Federal Housing Administration (FHA), part of HUD. Additional information can be found in Chapter 5 – "Home Loan Guaranty."

Life Insurance

National Guard members and reservists are eligible to receive Servicemembers' Group Life Insurance (SGLI), Veterans' Group Life Insurance (VGLI), and Family Servicemembers' Group Life Insurance (FSGLI). They may also be eligible for SGLI Traumatic Injury Protection if severely injured and suffering a qualifying loss, Service-Disabled Veterans Insurance if they receive a service-connected disability rating from VA, and Veterans' Mortgage Life Insurance if approved for a Specially Adapted Housing Grant. Complete details can be found in Chapter 6 – "VA Life Insurance."

Burial and Memorial Benefits

VA provides a burial flag to memorialize members or former members of the Selected Reserve who served their initial obligation, or were discharged for a disability incurred or aggravated in the line of duty, or died while a member of the Selected Reserve.

Reservists and National Guard members may be eligible for additional burial benefits if their death was due to an injury or disease that developed during, or was aggravated during, active duty, active duty for training, or inactive duty for training. Burial benefits may include burial in a national cemetery; an inscribed headstone, marker, or medallion; a Presidential Memorial Certificate; and an allowance to partially reimburse burial and funeral costs. Additional information about burial benefits that may be available can be found in Chapter 7 – "Burial and Memorial Benefits".

Re-employment Rights

A person who left a civilian job to enter active duty in the armed forces is entitled to return to the job after discharge or release from active duty if they:

1. Gave advance notice of military service to the employer.
2. Did not exceed five years cumulative absence from the civilian job (with some exceptions).
3. Submitted a timely application for re-employment.
4. Did not receive a dishonorable or other punitive discharge.

The law calls for a returning Veteran to be placed in the job as if he/she had never left, including benefits based on seniority such as pensions, pay increases and promotions. The law also prohibits discrimination in hiring, promotion or other advantages of employment on the basis of military service. Veterans seeking re-employment should apply, verbally or in writing, to the company's hiring official and keep a record of their application. If problems arise, contact the Department of Labor's Veterans' Employment and Training Service (VETS) in the state of the employer.

Federal employees not properly re-employed may appeal directly to the Merit Systems Protection Board. Non-federal employees may file complaints in U.S. District Court. For information, visit www.dol.gov/vets/programs/userra/main.htm.

Transition Assistance Advisor Program

The Transition Assistance Advisor (TAA) program is a partnership between the National Guard and VA to assist Veterans. The TAA Program, housed within the National Guard (NG) Office of Warrior Support, places a NG/VA trained expert at the NG Headquarters in each of the 50 states as well as PR, GU, VI, and the District of Columbia. The advisor serves as an advocate for Guard members and their families, as well as other geographically dispersed military members and families. In collaboration with state and local coalition partners, the TAA Program provides VA benefit enrollment assistance, referrals, and assists in facilitating access for Veterans through the overwhelming maze of programs, with the compassion of someone who knows what it is like to transition from the Guard to active duty and then back to civilian status.

Advisors receive annual training from VA experts in VA health care and benefits to assist Guard members and their families with access to VA health care facilities and TRICARE facilities within their network. To find a local Transition Assistance Advisor call 1-877-577-6691 or go to http://www.taapmo.com.

Outreach for OEF/OIF/New Dawn Veterans

VA's OEF/OIF/New Dawn Outreach Teams focus on improving outreach to members of the National Guard and Reserve by engaging them throughout the deployment cycle with targeted messages and face-to-face encounters with VA staff. These outreach teams are located at VA Medical Centers to help ease the transition from military to civilian life. To learn more, visit www.oefoif.va.gov. Veterans can also call the toll-free OEF/OIF/New Dawn Help Line at 1-866-606-8216 for answers to questions about VA benefits, health care, and enrollment procedures.

Air Reserve Personnel Center

The Air Reserve Personnel Center (ARPC) is available to assist with various personnel issues, including requests for personnel records, copies of DD Form 214, or other military documents. Many Veterans file an Air Force Board Correction of Military Records (AFBCMR) or write their Congressman to get these basic issues resolved, which requires that the request be routed through appropriate authorities, sometimes taking up to 180 days. Alternately, the ARPC routinely handles these actions on a much quicker basis. Members should call the ARPC for assistance at 1-800-525-0102 or logon to https://gum-crm.csd.disa.mil.

Chapter 10
Special Groups of Veterans

Homeless Veterans

VA's homeless programs constitute the largest integrated network of homeless assistance programs in the country, offering a wide array of services to help Veterans recover from homelessness and live as self-sufficiently and independently as possible.

The *VA Health Care for Homeless Veterans (HCHV) Program* provides a gateway to VA and community supportive services for eligible Veterans. Through the HCHV Program, Veterans are provided with case management and residential treatment in the community. The program also conducts outreach to homeless Veterans who are not likely to come to VA facilities on their own.

Homeless Veterans Supported Employment Program (HVSEP) provides vocational assistance, job development and placement, and ongoing employment supports designed to improve employment outcomes among homeless Veterans. HVSEP is coordinated between CWT and the continuum of Homeless Veterans Programs for the purpose of providing community-based vocational and employment services. All of the HVSEP vocational rehabilitation specialists (VRS) hired to provide employment services for the program consists of homeless, formerly homeless, or at risk of homelessness Veterans.

The **National Call Center for Homeless Veterans** (NCCHV) assists homeless Veterans, at-risk Veterans, their families and other interested parties with linkages to appropriate VA and community-based resources. The call center provides trained VA staff members 24 hours a day, seven days a week to assess a caller's needs and connect them to appropriate resources. The call center can be accessed by dialing 1-877-4AID VET (1-877-424-3838).

The **VA's Homeless Providers Grant and Per Diem Program** provides funds to non-profit community agencies providing transitional housing (up to 24 months) and/or offering services to homeless Veterans, such as case management, education, crisis intervention, counseling, and services targeted towards specialized populations including homeless women Veterans. The goal of the program is to help homeless Veterans achieve residential stability, increase their skill levels and/or income, and obtain greater self-determination.

The **Housing and Urban Development-Veterans Affairs Supportive Housing** (HUD-VASH) Program provides permanent housing and ongoing case management for eligible homeless Veterans who would not be able to live independently otherwise. This program allows eligible Veterans to live in Veteran-selected housing units with a "Housing Choice" voucher. These vouchers are portable to support the Veteran's choice of housing in communities served by their VA medical facility where case management services can be provided. HUD-VASH services include outreach and case management to ensure integration of services and continuity of care. This program enhances the ability of VA to serve homeless women Veterans, and homeless Veterans with families.

Through the **Supportive Services for Veteran Families Program**, VA aims to improve very low-income Veteran families' housing stability by providing supportive services in, or transitioning to, permanent housing. VA funds community-based organizations to provide eligible Veteran families with outreach, case management and assistance in obtaining VA and other benefits. Grantees may also provide time-limited payments to third parties (e.g., landlords, utility companies, moving companies and licensed child care providers) if these payments help Veterans' families stay in or acquire permanent housing on a sustainable basis.

In **VA's Compensated Work Therapy/Transitional Residence** (CWT/TR) Program, disadvantaged, at-risk, and homeless Veterans live in CWT/TR community-based supervised group homes while working for pay in VA's CWT Program, to learn new job skills, relearn successful work habits, and regain a sense of self-esteem and self-worth.

The **Health Care for Re-Entry Veterans (HCRV) Program** offers outreach, referrals and short-term case management assistance for incarcerated Veterans who may be at risk for homelessness upon their release.

For more information on VA homeless programs and services, Veterans currently enrolled in VA health care can speak with their VA mental health or health care provider. Other Veterans and interested parties can find a complete list of VA health care facilities at www. va.gov, or they can call VA's general information hotline at 1-800-827-1000. If assistance is needed when contacting a VA facility, ask to speak to the Health Care for Homeless Veterans Program or the Mental Health service manager. Information is also available on the VA Homeless program website at www.va.gov/homeless.

Filipino Veterans

World War II era Filipino Veterans are eligible for certain VA benefits. Generally, Old Philippine Scouts are eligible for VA benefits in the same manner as U.S. Veterans. Commonwealth Army Veterans, including certain organized Filipino guerrilla forces and New Philippine Scouts residing in the United States who are citizens or lawfully admitted for permanent residence, are also eligible for VA health care in the United States on the same basis as U.S. Veterans.

Certain Commonwealth Army Veterans and new Philippine Scouts may be eligible for disability compensation and burial benefits. Other Veterans of recognized guerrilla groups also may be eligible for certain VA benefits. Survivors of World War II era Filipino Veterans may be eligible for dependency and indemnity compensation. Eligibility and the rates of benefits vary based on the recipient's citizenship and place of residence. Call 1-800-827-1000 for additional information.

VA Benefits for Veterans Living Overseas

VA monetary benefits, including disability compensation, pension, educational benefits, and burial allowances are generally payable overseas. Some programs are restricted. Home loan guaranties are available only in the United States and selected U.S. territories and possessions. Educational benefits are limited to approved, degree-granting programs in institutions of higher learning. Beneficiaries living in foreign countries should contact the nearest American embassy or consulate for help. In Canada, contact an office of Veterans Affairs Canada. For information, visit http://www.vba.va.gov/bln/21/Foreign/index.htm.

World War II Era Merchant Marine Seamen

Certain Merchant Marine seamen who served in World War II may qualify for Veterans benefits. When applying for medical care, seamen must present their discharge certificate from the Department of Defense. Call 1-800-827-1000 for help obtaining a certificate.

Allied Veterans Who Served During WWI or WWII

VA may provide medical care to certain Veterans of nations allied or associated with the United States during World War I or World War II if authorized and reimbursed by the foreign government. VA also may provide hospitalization, outpatient care and domiciliary care to former members of the armed forces of Czechoslovakia or Poland who fought in World War I or World War II in armed conflict against an enemy of the United States if they have been U.S. citizens for at least 10 years.

World War Service by Particular Groups

A number of groups who provided military-related service to the United States can receive VA benefits. A discharge by the Secretary of Defense is needed to qualify. Service in the following groups has been certified as active military service for benefits purposes:

1. Women Air Force Service Pilots (WASPs).
2. World War I Signal Corps Female Telephone Operators Unit.
3. World War I Engineer Field Clerks.
4. Women's Army Auxiliary Corps (WAAC).
5. Quartermaster Corps female clerical employees serving with the American Expeditionary Forces in World War I.
6. Civilian employees of Pacific naval air bases who actively participated in defense of Wake Island during World War II.
7. Reconstruction aides and dietitians in World War I.
8. Male civilian ferry pilots.
9. Wake Island defenders from Guam.
10. Civilian personnel assigned to OSS secret intelligence.
11. Guam Combat Patrol.
12. Quartermaster Corps members of the Keswick crew on Corregidor during World War II.
13. U.S. civilians who participated in the defense of Bataan.
14. U.S. merchant seamen on block ships in support of Operation Mulberry in the World War II invasion of Normandy.
15. American merchant marines in oceangoing service during World War II.
16. Civilian Navy IFF radar technicians who served in combat areas of the Pacific during World War II.
17. U.S. civilians of the American Field Service who served overseas in World War I.
18. U.S. civilians of the American Field Service who served overseas under U.S. armies and U.S. army groups in World War II.

19. U.S. civilian employees of American Airlines who served overseas in a contract with the Air Transport Command between Dec. 14, 1941, and Aug. 14, 1945.

20. Civilian crewmen of U.S. Coast and Geodetic Survey vessels who served in areas of immediate military hazard while conducting cooperative operations with and for the U.S. armed forces between Dec. 7, 1941, and Aug. 15, 1945 Qualifying vessels are: the Derickson, Explorer, Gilber, Hilgard, E. Lester Jones, Lydonia Patton, Surveyor, Wainwright, Westdahl, Oceanographer, Hydrographer and Pathfinder.

21. Members of the American Volunteer Group (Flying Tigers) who served between Dec. 7, 1941, and July 18, 1942.

22. U.S. civilian flight crew and aviation ground support employees of United Air Lines who served overseas in a contract with Air Transport Command between Dec. 14, 1941, and Aug.14, 1945.

23. U.S. civilian flight crew, including pursers, and aviation ground support employees of Transcontinental and Western Air, Inc. who served overseas in a contract with the Air Transport Command between Dec. 14, 1941, and Aug. 14, 1945.

24. U.S. civilian flight crew and aviation ground support employees of Consolidated Vultee Aircraft Corp. who served overseas in a contract with Air Transport Command between Dec. 14, 1941, and Aug. 14, 1945.

25. U.S. civilian flight crew and aviation ground support employees of Pan American World Airways and its subsidiaries and affiliates, who served overseas in a contract with the Air Transport Command and Naval Air Transport Service between Dec. 14, 1941, and Aug. 14, 1945.

26. Honorably discharged members of the American Volunteer Guard, Eritrea Service Command, between June 21, 1942, and March 31, 1943.

27. U.S. civilian flight crew and aviation ground support employees of Northwest Airlines who served overseas under the airline's contract with Air Transport Command from Dec. 14, 1941, through Aug. 14, 1945.

28. U.S. civilian female employees of the U.S. Army Nurse Corps who served in the defense of Bataan and Corregidor between Jan. 2, 1942, and Feb. 3, 1945.

29. U.S. flight crew and aviation ground support employees of

Northeast Airlines Atlantic Division, who served overseas as a result of Northeast Airlines' contract with the Air Transport Command from Dec. 7, 1941, through Aug. 14, 1945.

30. U.S. civilian flight crew and aviation ground support employees of Braniff Airways, who served overseas in the North Atlantic or under the jurisdiction of the North Atlantic Wing, Air Transport Command, as a result of a contract with the Air Transport Command between Feb. 26, 1945, and Aug. 14, 1945.

31. Chamorro and Carolina former native police who received military training in the Donnal area of central Saipan and were placed under command of Lt. Casino of the 6th Provisional Military Police Battalion to accompany U.S. Marines on active, combat patrol from Aug. 19, 1945, to Sept. 2, 1945.

32. Three scouts/guides, Miguel Tenorio, Penedicto Taisacan, and Cristino Dela Cruz, who assisted the United States Marines in the offensive operations against the Japanese on the Northern Mariana Islands from June 19, 1944, through Sept. 2, 1945.

33. The operational Analysis Group of the Office of Scientific Research and Development, Office of Emergency Management, which served overseas with the U.S. Army Air Corps from Dec. 7, 1941, through Aug. 15, 1945.

34. Service as a member of the Alaska Territorial Guard during World War II or any individual who was honorably discharged under section 8147 of the Department of Defense Appropriations Act of 2001.

Incarcerated Veterans

VA benefits are affected if a beneficiary is convicted of a felony and imprisoned for more than 60 days. Disability or death pension paid to an incarcerated beneficiary must be discontinued. Disability compensation paid to an incarcerated Veteran rated 20 percent or more disabled is limited to the 10 percent rate. For a Veteran whose disability rating is 10 percent, the payment is reduced to half of the rate payable to a Veteran evaluated as 10 percent disabled.

Any amounts not paid to the Veteran while incarcerated may be apportioned to eligible dependents. Payments are not reduced for participants in work-release programs, residing in halfway houses or under community control.

Failure to notify VA of a Veteran's incarceration can result in overpayment of benefits and the subsequent loss of all VA financial benefits until the overpayment is recovered. VA benefits will not be provided to any Veteran or dependent wanted for an outstanding felony warrant.

The Health Care for Reentry Veterans Program (HCRV) offers outreach to Veterans incarcerated in state and federal prisons, and referrals and short-term case management assistance upon release from prison.

The Veterans Justice Outreach Program (VJO) offers outreach and case management to Veterans involved in law enforcement encounters, overseen by treatment courts, and incarcerated in local jails. Visit www.va.gov/homeless/ to locate an outreach worker.

Chapter 11
Transition Assistance

Joint Transition Assistance

The Departments of Veterans Affairs, Defense, and Labor relaunched a new and improved website for wounded warriors – the National Resource Directory (NRD). This directory (www.nrd.gov) provides access to thousands of services and resources at the national, state and local levels to support recovery, rehabilitation and community reintegration. The NRD is a comprehensive online tool available nationwide for wounded, ill and injured Servicemembers, Veterans and their families.

The NRD includes extensive information for Veterans seeking resources on VA benefits such as disability benefits, pensions for Veterans and their families, VA health care insurance and the GI Bill. The NRD's design and interface is simple, easy-to-navigate and intended to answer the needs of a broad audience of users within the military, Veteran and caregiver communities.

Transition From Military to VA

VA has personnel stationed at major military hospitals to help seriously injured Servicemembers returning from Operations Enduring Freedom, Iraqi Freedom, and New Dawn (OEF/OIF/OND) as they transition from military to civilian life. OEF/OIF Servicemembers who have questions about VA benefits or need assistance in filing a VA claim or accessing services can contact the nearest VA office or call 1-800-827-1000.

eBenefits

The eBenefits portal (www.ebenefits.va.gov) provides Servicemembers, Veterans, their families, and Caregivers with self-service access to benefit applications, benefits information, and access to personal information such as official military personnel file documents. The portal provides two main services; it catalogs links to information on other websites about military and Veteran benefits, and it provides a personalized workspace called My Dashboard, which gives quick access to all the online tools currently integrated into eBenefits.

Transition Assistance Program:consists of comprehensive work-shops at military installations designed to assist Servicemembers as they transition from military to civilian life. The program includes job search, employment and training information, as well as VA benefits information for Servicemembers who are within 18 months of sepa-ration or retirement. The VA Benefit Briefings are comprised of two briefings focusing on education, benefits. and VA health care and dis-ability compensation. Servicemembers can sign up for one-on-one appointments with a VA representative. Interested Servicemembers should contact their local TAP Manager to sign up for this program.

VOW to Hire Heroes Act
Improving the Transition Assistance Program (TAP): The VOW to Hire Heroes Act of 2011 ("the Act") made TAP, including attendance at the VA Benefit Briefings, mandatory for most Servicemembers transitioning to civilian status, upgraded career counseling options, and tailored TAP for the 21st Century job market.

Facilitating Seamless Transition: The Act allows Servicemembers to begin the federal employment process prior to separation in order to facilitate a truly seamless transition from the military to jobs at VA, Department of Homeland Security, and the many other federal agen-cies seeking to hire Veterans.

Expanding Education and Training: The Act provides nearly 100,000 unemployed Veterans of past eras and wars with up to one year of assistance (equal to the full-time payment rate under the Montgomery GI Bill-Active Duty program) to qualify for jobs in high-demand sectors. It also provides disabled Veterans up to one year of additional Vocational Rehabilitation and Employment benefits.

Translating Military Skills and Training: The Act requires the Department of Labor take a hard look at military skills and training equivalencies that are transferrable to the civilian sector and make it easier to obtain licenses and certifications.

Veterans Tax Credits: The Act provides tax credits for hiring Veter-ans and disabled Veterans who are out of work.

The inTransition
Servicemembers and Veterans may receive assistance from the in-Transition Program when they are receiving mental health treatment

and are making transitions from military service, location or a health care system. This program provides access to transitional support, motivation, and healthy lifestyle assistance and advice from qualified coaches through the toll-free telephone number 1-800-424-7877. For more information about The inTransition Program, please log onto www.health.mil/inTransition.

Pre-Discharge Program
The Pre-Discharge Program is a joint VA and DoD program that affords Servicemembers the opportunity to file claims for disability compensation and other benefits up to 180 days prior to separation or retirement.

The two primary components of the Pre-Discharge Program, Benefits Delivery at Discharge (BDD) and Quick Start, may be utilized by separating and retiring Servicemembers on active duty, including members of the Coast Guard, and members of the National Guard and Reserves (activated under Titles 10 or 32) in CONUS and some overseas locations. BDD is offered to accelerate receipt of VA disability benefits after release or discharge from active duty.

To participate in the BDD program, Servicemembers must:
1. have at least 60 days, but not more than 180 days, remaining on active duty.
2. have a known date of separation or retirement.
3. provide VA with service treatment records, originals or photocopies.
4. be available to complete all necessary examinations prior to leaving the point of separation.

Quick Start is offered to Servicemembers who have less than 60 days remaining on active duty or are unable to complete the necessary examinations prior to leaving the point of separation.

To participate in the Quick Start Program, Servicemembers must:
1. have at least one day remaining on active duty.
2. have a known date of separation or retirement.
3. provide VA with service treatment records, originals or photocopies.

Servicemembers should contact the local Transition Assistance Office or Army Career Alumni Program Center to schedule appointments to attend VA benefits briefings and learn how to initiate a pre-discharge claim. Servicemembers can obtain more information by calling VA toll-free at 1-800-827-1000 or by visiting www.vba.va.gov/predischarge.

Integrated Disability Evaluation System (IDES)
A third component of the Pre-Discharge program is the Integrated Disability Evaluation System. The IDES program covers Service-members who are referred to a Medical Evaluation Board.
The IDES program has three goals:
    1. a single seiers of disability exams conducted to VA standards that is used by both Departments;
    2. a single disability rating completed by VA that is binding upon both Departments; and
    3. expeditious payment of VA benefits after a Servicemember's separation from service.

VA Form 21-0819, VA/DoD Joint Disability Evaluation Board Claim, is initiated by the Military Service Coordinator jointly with Servicemem-ber (SM), when the SM is initially referred to IDES. The VA Form 21-0819, will not only reflect the military referred/unfitting medical conditions, but all claimed medical conditions affecting the uniformed member. This approach provides a comprehensive view of the SM's health at the time of the IDES evaluation process.

Federal Recovery Coordination Program
The Federal Recovery Coordination Program (FRCP), a joint pro-gram of DoD and VA, helps coordinate and access federal, state and local programs, benefits and services for seriously wounded, ill, and injured Servicemembers, and their families through recovery, reha-bilitation, and reintegration into the community.

Federal Recovery Coordinators (FRCs) have the delegated author-ity for oversight and coordination of the clinical and non-clinical care identified in each client's Federal Individual Recovery Plan (FIRP). Working with a variety of case managers, FRCs assist their clients in reaching their FIRP goals. FRCs remain with their clients as long as they are needed regardless of the client's location, duty or health status. In doing so, they often serve as the central point of contact and provide transition support for their clients.
Military Services Provide Pre-Separation Counseling
Servicemembers may receive pre-separation counseling 24 months

prior to retirement or 12 months prior to separation from active duty. These sessions present information on education, training, employment assistance, National Guard and Reserve programs, medical benefits, and financial assistance.

Verification of Military Experience and Training
The Verification of Military Experience and Training (VMET) Document, DD Form 2586, helps Servicemembers verify previous experience and training to potential employers, negotiate credits at schools, and obtain certificates or licenses. VMET documents are available only through each military branch support offices and are intended for Servicemembers who have at least six months of active service. Servicemembers should obtain VMET documents from their Transition Support Office within 12 months of separation or 24 months of retirement.

Transition Bulletin Board
To find business opportunities, a calendar of transition seminars, job fairs, information on Veterans associations, transition services, training and education opportunities, as well as other announcements at www.turbotap.org

DoD Transportal
To find locations and phone numbers of all Transition Assistance Offices as well as mini-courses on conducting successful job-search campaigns, writing resumes, using the internet to find a job, and links to job search and recruiting Websites, visit the DoD Transportal at www.Veteranprograms.com/index.html

Educational and Vocational Counseling
The Vocational Rehabilitation and Employment (VR&E) Program provides educational and vocational counseling to Servicemembers, Veterans, and certain dependents (U.S.C. Title 38, Section 3697) at no charge. These counseling services are designed to help an individual choose a vocational direction, determine the course needed to achieve the chosen goal, and evaluate the career possibilities open to them.

Assistance may include interest and aptitude testing, occupational exploration, setting occupational goals, locating the right type of training program, and exploring educational or training facilities which can be utilized to achieve an occupational goal.

Counseling services include, but are not limited to, educational and vocational counseling and guidance; testing; analysis of and recommendations to improve job-marketing skills; identification of employment, training, and financial aid resources; and referrals to other agencies providing these services.

Eligibility: Educational and vocational counseling services are available during the period the individual is on active duty with the armed forces and within 180 days of the estimated date of his or her discharge or release from active duty. The projected discharge must be under conditions other than dishonorable.

Servicemembers are eligible even if they are only considering whether or not they will continue as members of the armed forces. Veterans are eligible if not more than one year has elapsed since the date they were last discharged or released from active duty.

Veterans and dependents who are eligible for VA education benefits may receive educational and vocational counseling at any time during their eligibility period. This service is based on having eligibility for a VA program such as Chapter 30 (Montgomery GI Bill); Chapter 31 (Vocational Rehabilitation and Employment); Chapter 32 (Veterans Education Assistance Program – VEAP); Chapter 33 (Post-9/11 GI Bill); Chapter 35 (Dependents' Educational Assistance Program) for certain spouses and dependent children; Chapter 18 (Spina Bifida Program) for certain dependent children; and Chapter 1606 and 1607 of Title 10.

Veterans and Servicemembers may apply for counseling services using VA Form 28-8832, Application for Counseling. Veterans and Servicemembers may also write a letter expressing a desire for counseling services.

Upon receipt of either type of request for counseling from an eligible individual, an appointment for counseling will be scheduled. Counseling services are provided to eligible persons at no charge.

Veterans' Workforce Investment Program
Recently separated Veterans and those with service-connected disabilities, significant barriers to employment or who served on active duty during a period in which a campaign or expedition badge was authorized can contact the nearest state employment office for em-

ployment help through the Veterans Workforce Investment Program. The program may be conducted through state or local public agencies, community organizations or private, nonprofit organizations.

State Employment Services
Veterans can find employment information, education and training opportunities, job counseling, job search workshops, and resume preparation assistance at state Workforce Career or One-Stop Centers. These offices also have specialists to help disabled Veterans find employment.

Unemployment Compensation
Veterans who do not begin civilian employment immediately after leaving military service may receive weekly unemployment compensation for a limited time. The amount and duration of payments are determined by individual states. Apply by contacting the nearest state employment office listed in the local telephone directory.

Veterans Preference for Federal Jobs
Since the time of the Civil War, Veterans of the U.S. armed forces have been given some degree of preference in appointments to federal jobs. Veterans' preference in its present form comes from the Veterans' Preference Act of 1944, as amended, and now codified in Title 5, United States Code. By law, Veterans who are disabled or who served on active duty in the U.S. armed forces during certain specified time periods or in military campaigns are entitled to preference over others when hiring from competitive lists of eligible candidates, and also in retention during a reduction in force (RIF).

To receive preference, a Veteran must have been discharged or released from active duty in the U.S. armed forces under honorable conditions (honorable or general discharge). Preference is also provided for certain widows and widowers of deceased Veterans who died in service; spouses of service-connected disabled Veterans; and mothers of Veterans who died under honorable conditions on active duty or have permanent and total service-connected disabilities. For each of these preferences, there are specific criteria that must be met in order to be eligible to receive the Veterans' preference.

Recent changes in Title 5 clarify Veterans preference eligibility criteria for National Guard and Reserve members. Veterans eligible for preference include Reservists and National Guard members who served on active duty as defined by Title 38 at any time in the armed forces for a period of more than 180 consecutive days, any part of which occurred during the period beginning on Sept. 11, 2001, and ending on the date prescribed by Presidential proclamation or by law as the last date of OEF/OIF. Reservists and National Guardsmen must have been discharged or released from active duty in the armed forces under honorable conditions.

Another recent change involves Veterans who earned the Global War on Terrorism Expeditionary Medal for service in OEF/OIF/OND. Under Title 5, service on active duty in the armed forces during a war or in a campaign or expedition for which a campaign badge has been authorized also qualifies for Veterans preference. Any Armed Forces Expeditionary medal or campaign badge qualifies for preference. Medal holders must have served continuously for 24 months or the full period called or ordered to active duty. For additional information, visit the Office of Personnel Management (OPM) website at www. fedshirevets.gov.

In 2011, President Obama signed the VOW (Veterans Opportunity to Work) To Hire Heroes Act. VOW amends Chapter 21 of Title 5, United States Code (U.S.C.) by adding section 2108a, "Treatment of certain individuals as Veterans, disabled Veterans, and preference eligibles." Section 2108a requires Federal agencies to treat active duty Servicemembers as Veterans, disabled Veterans, or preference eligibles for purposes of appointment in the competitive service when these Servicemembers submit a certification of expected discharge or release from active duty under honorable conditions along with their applications for Federal employment. A certification is any written document from the armed forces that certifies the Servicemember is expected to be discharged or released from active duty service in the armed forces under honorable conditions not later than 120 days from the date the certification is signed.

Veterans' preference does not require an agency to use any particular appointment process. Agencies can pick candidates from a number of different special hiring authorities or through a variety of different sources. For example, the agency can reinstate a former federal employee, transfer someone from another agency, reassign someone from within the agency, make a selection under merit promotion procedures or through open, competitive exams, or appoint someone noncompetitively under special authority such as a Veterans Readjustment Appointment or special authority for 30 percent or more disabled Veterans. The decision on which hiring authority the agency desires to use rests solely with the agency. When applying for federal jobs, eligible Veterans should claim preference on their application or resume. Veterans should apply for a federal job by contacting the personnel office at the agency in which they wish to work. For more information, visit www.usajobs.gov for job openings or help creating a federal resume.

Veterans' Employment Opportunities Act: When an agency accepts applications from outside its own workforce, the Veterans' Employment Opportunities Act of 1998 allows preference eligible candidates or Veterans to compete for these vacancies under merit promotion procedures.Veterans who are selected are given career or career-conditional appointments. Veterans are those who have been separated under honorable conditions from the U.S. armed forces with three or more years of continuous active service. For information, visit www.usajobs.gov or www.fedshirevets.gov.

Veterans' Recruitment Appointment: Allows federal agencies to appoint eligible Veterans to jobs without competition. These appointments can be converted to career or career-conditional positions after two years of satisfactory work. Veterans should apply directly to the agency where they wish to work. For information,www.fedshirevets.gov/.

Small Businesses
VA's Center for Veterans Enterprise helps Veterans interested in forming or expanding small businesses and helps VA contracting offices identify Veteran-owned small businesses. For information, write the U.S. Department of Veterans Affairs (OOVE), 810 Vermont Avenue, N.W., Washington, DC 20420-0001, call toll-free 1-866-584-2344 or visit www.vetbiz.gov. Small Business Contracts: Like other federal agencies, VA is required to place a portion of its contracts and purchases with small and disadvantaged businesses. VA has a special office to help small and disadvantaged businesses get information on VA acquisition opportunities. For information, write the U.S. Department of Veterans Affairs (OOSB), 810 Vermont Avenue, N.W., Washington, DC 20420-0001, call toll-free 1-800-949-8387 or visit www.va.gov/osdbu/.

Chapter 12

Dependents and Survivors Health Care

Civilian Health and Medical Program of the Department of Veterans Affairs (CHAMPVA). Under CHAMPVA, certain dependents and survivors can receive reimbursement for most medical expenses – inpatient, outpatient, mental health, prescription medication, skilled nursing care and durable medical equipment.

Eligibility: To be eligible for CHAMPVA, an individual cannot be eligible for TRICARE (the medical program for civilian dependents provided by DoD) and must be one of the following:
1. The spouse or child of a Veteran whom VA has rated permanently and totally disabled due to a service-connected disability.
2. The surviving spouse or child of a Veteran who died from a VA-rated service-connected disability, or who, at the time of death, was rated permanently and totally disabled.
3. The surviving spouse or child of a Veteran who died on active duty service and in the line of duty, not due to misconduct. However, in most of these cases, these family members are eligible for TRI-CARE, not CHAMPVA.

A surviving spouse under age 55 who remarries loses CHAMPVA eligibility at midnight of the date on remarriage. He/she may re-establish eligibility if the remarriage ends by death, divorce or annulment effective the first day of the month following the termination of the remarriage or Dec. 1, 1999, whichever is later. A surviving spouse who remarries after age 55 does not lose eligibility upon remarriage.

For those who have Medicare entitlement or other health insurance, CHAMPVA is a secondary payer. Beneficiaries with Medicare must be enrolled in Parts A&B to maintain CHAMPVA eligibility. For additional information, contact Purchased Care at the VA Health Administration Center, CHAMPVA, P.O. Box 469028, Denver, CO 80246, call 1-800-733-8387 or visit www.va.gov/hac/forbeneficiaries/champva/champva.asp.

Many VA health care facilities provide services to CHAMPVA beneficiaries under the CHAMPVA In-house Treatment Initiative (CITI) program. Contact the nearest VA health care facility to determine if it participates. Those who use a CITI facility incur no cost for services; however, services are provided on a space-available basis, after the needs of Veterans are met. Not all services are available at all times. The coverage of services is dependent upon the CHAMPVA benefit coverage. CHAMPVA beneficiaries who are covered by Medicare cannot use CITI.

VA's Comprehensive Assistance for Family Caregivers Program entitles the designated Primary Family Caregiver, who is without health insurance coverage, CHAMPVA benefits. Some of the health plans that would make a Primary Family Caregiver ineligible for CHAMPVA benefits include Medicare, Medicaid, commercial health plans through employment and individual plans.

Children Born with Spina Bifida to Certain Vietnam or Korea Veterans: The Spina Bifida Program (SB) is a comprehensive health care benefits program administered by the Department of Veterans Affairs for birth children of certain Vietnam and Korea Veterans who have been diagnosed with spina bifida (except spina bifida occulta). The SB program provides reimbursement for inpatient and outpatient medical services, pharmacy, durable medical equipment, and supplies. Purchased Care at the VA's Health Administration Center in Denver, Colorado manages the SB Program, including the authorization of benefits and the subsequent processing and payment of claims. For more information about spina bifida health care benefits, call 1-888-820-1756 or visit www.va.gov/hac/forbeneficiaries/spina/spina.asp

Eligibility: To be eligible for the SB Program, Veterans must be eligible for a monetary award under the Veterans Benefits Administration (VBA). The Denver VA Regional Office makes the determination regarding this entitlement. The VBA notifies Purchased Care at the VA Health Administration Center after an award is made and the eligible child is enrolled in SB.

Children of Women Vietnam Veterans (CWVV) Born with Certain Birth Defects: The CWVV Health Care Program is a federal health benefits program administered by the Department of Veterans Affairs for children of women Vietnam Veterans born with certain birth defects. The CWVV Program provides reimbursement for medical care related to covered birth defects and conditions associated with the covered birth defect except for spina bifida. For more information about benefits for children with birth defects, call 1-888-820-1756 or visit www.va.gov/hac/forbeneficiaries and select Spina Bifida/Children of Women Vietnam Veterans (CWVV.)

Eligibility: To be eligible for the CWVV Program, Veterans must have received an award under VBA. The Denver VA Regional Office makes determination regarding this entitlement. The VBA notifies Purchased Care at the VA Health Administration Center after an award is made and the eligible child is enrolled in CWVV.

Bereavement Counseling: VA Vet Centers provide bereavement counseling to all family members including spouses, children, parents, and siblings of Servicemembers who die while on active duty. This includes federally activated members of the National Guard and reserve components. Bereavement services may be accessed by calling (202) 461-6530.

Bereavement Counseling related to Veterans: Bereavement counseling is available through any VA medical center to immediate family members of Veterans who die unexpectedly or while participating in a VA hospice or similar program, as long as the immediate family members had been receiving family support services in connection with or in furtherance of the Veteran's treatment. (In other cases, bereavement counseling is available to the Veteran's legal guardian or the individual with whom the Veteran had certified an intention to live, as long as the guardian or individual had been receiving covered family support services.) This bereavement counseling is of limited duration and may only be authorized up to 60 days. However, VA medical center directors have authority to approve a longer period of time when medically indicated. Contact the Social Work Service at the nearest VA medical center to access bereavement counseling.

Chapter 13
Dependents and Survivors Benefits

Death Gratuity Payment

Military services provide payment, called a death gratuity, in the amount of $100,000 to the next of kin of Servicemembers who die while on active duty (including those who die within 120 days of separation) as a result of service-connected injury or illness.

If there is no surviving spouse or child, then parents or siblings designated as next of kin by the Servicemember may be provided the payment. The payment is made by the last military command of the deceased. If the beneficiary is not paid automatically, application may be made to the military service concerned.

Dependency and Indemnity Compensation

Eligibility: For a survivor to be eligible for Dependency and Indemnity Compensation (DIC), one of the following must have directly caused or contributed to the Veteran's death:

1. A disease or injury incurred or aggravated in the line of duty while on active duty or active duty for training.
2. An injury, heart attack, cardiac arrest, or stroke incurred or aggravated in the line of duty while on inactive duty for training.
3. A service-connected disability or a condition directly related to a service-connected disability.

DIC also may be paid to certain survivors of Veterans who were totally disabled from service-connected conditions at the time of death, even though their service-connected disabilities did not cause their deaths. The survivor qualifies if the Veteran was:

1. Continuously rated totally disabled for a period of 10 years immediately preceding death; or
2. Continuously rated totally disabled from the date of military discharge and for at least 5 years immediately preceding death; or
3. A former POW who was continuously rated totally disabled for a period of at least on a year immediately preceding death.

Payments will be offset by any amount received from judicial proceedings brought on by the Veteran's death. When the surviving spouse is eligible for payments under the military's Survivor Benefit Plan (SBP), only the amount of SBP greater than DIC is payable. If DIC is greater than SBP, only DIC is payable. The Veteran's discharge must have been under conditions other than dishonorable.

Payments for Deaths After Jan. 1, 1993: Surviving spouses of Veterans who died on or after Jan. 1, 1993, receive a basic rate, plus additional payments for dependent children, for the aid and attendance of another person if they are patients in a nursing home or require the regular assistance of another person, or if they are permanently housebound.

Aid and Attendance and Housebound Benefits

Surviving Surviving spouses who are eligible for DIC or survivors pension may also be eligible for Aid and Attendance or Housebound benefits. They may apply for these benefits by writing to their VA regional office. They should include copies of any evidence, preferably a report from an attending physician or a nursing home, validating the need for aid and attendance or housebound care. The report should contain sufficient detail to determine whether there is disease or injury producing physical or mental impairment, loss of coordination, or conditions affecting the ability to dress and undress, to feed oneself, to attend to sanitary needs, and to keep oneself ordinarily clean and presentable. In addition, it is necessary to determine whether the surviving spouse is confined to the home or immediate premises.

2013 DIC Payment Rates for Surviving Spouses

DIC rates (Veteran died on or after Jan. 1, 1993.)

Allowances	Monthly Rate
Basic Payment Rate	$1,215
Additional Allowances:	
Each Dependent Child	$301
Aid and Attendance	$301
Housebound	$141

Special Allowances: Add $258 if the Veteran was totally disabled eight continuous years prior to death.

Add $263 to the additional allowance if there are dependent children under age 18 for the initial two years of entitlement for DIC awards commencing on or after Jan. 1, 2005.

Payments for Deaths Prior to Jan. 1, 1993: Surviving spouses of Veterans who died prior to Jan. 1, 1993, receive an amount based on the deceased's military pay grade.

DIC Rates (Veteran who died prior to Jan. 1, 1993)

Enlisted	Rate	Warrant Officer	Rate	Officer	Rate
E-1	$1,215	W-1	$1,283	O-1	$1,283
E-2	$1,215	W-2	$1,334	O-2	$1,327
E-3	$1,215	W-3	$1,373	O-3	$1,418
E-4	$1,215	W-4	$1,453	O-4	$1,503
E-5	$1,215			O-5	$1,654
E-6	$1,215			O-6	$1,865
E-7	$1,257			O-7	$2,013
E-8	$1,327			O-8	$2,211
E-9	$1,384			O-9	$2,365
				O-10	$2,594

Parents' DIC: VA provides an income-based monthly benefit to the surviving parent(s) of a Servicemember or Veteran whose death was service-related. When countable income exceeds the limit set by law, no benefits are payable. The spouse's income must also be included if living with a spouse.

A spouse may be the other parent of the deceased Veteran, or a spouse from remarriage. Unreimbursed medical expenses may be used to reduce countable income. Benefit rates and income limits change annually.

Restored Entitlement Program for Survivors: Survivors of Veterans who died of service-connected causes incurred or aggravated prior to Aug. 13, 1981, may be eligible for a special benefit payable in addition to any other benefits to which the family may be entitled. The amount of the benefit is based on information provided by the Social Security Administration.

Survivors Pension

VA provides pension benefits to qualifying surviving spouses and unmarried children of deceased Veterans with wartime service.

Eligibility: To be eligible, spouses must not have remarried and children must be under age 18, or under age 23 if attending a VA-approved school, or have become permanently incapable of self-support because of disability before age 18. Surviving spouses and children must have qualifying income.

The Veteran must have been discharged under conditions other than dishonorable and must have had 90 days or more of active military service, at least one day of which was during a period of war, or a service-connected disability justifying discharge. Longer periods of service may be required for Veterans who entered active duty on or after Sept. 8, 1980, or Oct. 16, 1981, if an officer. If the Veteran died in service but not in the line of duty, survivors pension may be payable if the Veteran completed at least two years of honorable service.

Children who become incapable of self-support because of a disability before age 18 may be eligible for survivors pension as long as the condition exists, unless the child marries or the child's income exceeds the applicable limit.

Payment: Survivors pension provides a monthly payment to bring an eligible person's income to a level established by law. The payment is reduced by the annual income from other sources such as Social Security. The payment may be increased if the recipient has unreimbursed medical expenses that can be deducted from countable income.

Aid and Attendance and Housebound Benefits

Surviving spouses who are eligible for VA survivors pension are eligible for a higher maximum pension rate if they qualify for aid and attendance or housebound benefits. An eligible individual may qualify if he or she requires the regular aid of another person in order to perform personal functions required for everyday living, or is bedridden, a patient in a nursing home due to mental or physical incapacity, blind, or permanently and substantially confined to his/her immediate premises because of a disability.

Surviving spouses who are ineligible for basic survivors pension based on annual income may still be eligible for survivors pension if they are eligible for aid and attendance or housebound benefits because a higher income limit applies. In addition, unreimbursed medical expenses for nursing-home or home-health care may be used to reduce countable annual income, which may result in a higher pension benefit.

To apply for aid and attendance or housebound benefits, write to a VA regional office. Please include copies of any evidence, preferably a report from an attending physician or a nursing home, validating the need for aid and attendance or housebound type care. The report should contain sufficient detail to determine whether there is disease or injury producing physical or mental impairment, loss of coordination, or conditions affecting the ability to dress and undress, to feed oneself, to attend to sanitary needs, and to keep oneself ordinarily clean and presentable. In addition, it is necessary to determine whether the claimant is confined to the home or immediate premises.

2013 Survivors Pension Rates

Recipient of Pension	Maximum Annual Rate
Surviving spouse	$8,359
(With dependent child)	$10,942
Permanently housebound	$10,217
(With dependent child)	$12,796
Needs regular aid & attendance	$13,362
(With dependent child)	$15,940
Each additional dependent child	$2,129
Pension for each surviving child	$2,129

Survivors' & Dependents' Educational Assistance
Eligibility: VA provides educational assistance to qualifying dependents as follows:
 1. The spouse or child of a Servicemember or Veteran who either died of a service-connected disability, or who has permanent and total service-connected disability, or who died while such a disability existed.
 2. The spouse or child of a Servicemember listed for more than 90 days as currently Missing in Action (MIA), captured in the line of duty by a hostile force, or detained or interned by a

foreign government or power.
3. The spouse or child of a Servicemember who is hospitalized
   or receives outpatient care or treatment for a disability that
   is determined to be totally and permanently disabling, incurred
   or aggravated due to active duty, and for which the service
   member is likely to be discharged from military service.

Surviving spouses lose eligibility if they remarry before age 57 or are living with another person who has been recognized publicly as their spouse. They can regain eligibility if their remarriage ends by death or divorce or if they cease living with the person. Dependent children do not lose eligibility if the surviving spouse remarries. Visit www. gibill.va.gov/ for more information.

Period of Eligibility: The period of eligibility for Veterans' spouses expires 10 years from either the date they become eligible or the date of the Veteran's death. Children generally must be between the ages of 18 and 26 to receive educational benefits. VA may grant extensions to both spouses and children.

The period of eligibility for spouses of Servicemembers who died on active duty expires 20 years from the date of death. This is a change in law that became effective Dec. 10, 2004. Spouses of Servicemembers who died on active duty whose 10-year eligibility period expired before Dec. 10, 2004, now have 20 years from the date of death to use educational benefits. Effective Oct. 10, 2008, Public Law 110-389 provides a 20-year period of eligibility for spouses of Veterans with a permanent and total service-connected disability rating effective within 3 years of release from active duty.

Payments: The payment rate effective Oct. 1, 2012, is $987 a month for full-time school attendance, with lesser amounts for part-time. Benefits are paid for full-time training up to 45 months or the equivalent in part-time training.

Training Available: Benefits may be awarded for pursuit of associate, bachelor, or graduate degrees at colleges and universities; independent study; cooperative training study abroad certificate or diploma from business, technical or vocational schools, apprenticeships, on-the-job training programs; farm cooperative courses; and preparatory courses for tests required or used for admission to an institution of higher learning or graduate school. Benefits for correspondence courses under certain conditions are available to spouses only. Beneficiaries without high-school degrees can pursue secondary schooling, and those with a deficiency in a subject may receive tutorial assistance if enrolled half-time or more.

Special Benefits: Dependents over age 14 with physical or mental disabilities that impair their ability to pursue an education may receive specialized vocational or restorative training, including speech and voice correction, language retraining, lip reading, auditory training, Braille reading and writing, and similar programs. Certain disabled or surviving spouses are also eligible.

Marine Gunnery Sergeant John David Fry Scholarship
Children of those who died in the line of duty on or after Sept. 11, 2001, are potentially eligible to use Post-9/11 GI Bill benefits. Refer to Chapter 4, "Education and Training", for more details.

Work-Study: See page 55

Counseling: VA may provide counseling to help participants pursue an educational or vocational objective.

Montgomery GI Bill (MGIB) Death Benefit: VA will pay a special MGIB death benefit to a designated survivor in the event of the service-connected death of a Servicemember while on active duty or within one year after discharge or release. The deceased must either have been entitled to educational assistance under the MGIB program or a participant in the program who would have been so entitled but for the high school diploma or length-of-service requirement. The amount paid will be equal to the participant's actual military pay reduction, less any education benefits paid.

Children of Veterans Born with Certain Birth Defects Children of Vietnam or Korean Veterans Born with Spina Bifida: Biological children of male and female Veterans who served in Vietnam at any time during the period beginning Jan. 9, 1962 and ending May 7, 1975, or who served in or near the Korean demilitarized zone (DMZ) during the period beginning Sept. 1, 1967 and ending Aug. 31, 1971, born with spina bifida may be eligible for a monthly monetary allowance, and vocational training if reasonably feasible.
The law defines "child" as the natural child of a Vietnam Veteran, regardless of age or marital status. The child must have been con-

ceived after the date on which the Veteran first entered the Republic of Vietnam. For more information about benefits for children with birth defects, visit www.va.gov/hac/forbeneficiaries/spina/spina.asp.

A monetary allowance is paid at one of three disability levels based on the neurological manifestations that define the severity of disability: impairment of the functioning of extremities, impairment of bowel or bladder function, and impairment of intellectual functioning.

2012 VA Benefits for Children of Vietnam or Korean Veterans Born with Spina Bifida

	Level I	Level II	Level III
Monthly Rate	$303	$1,038	$1,769

Children of Women Vietnam Veterans Born with Certain Birth Defects: Biological children of women Veterans who served in Vietnam at any time during the period beginning on Feb. 28, 1961 and ending on May 7, 1975, may be eligible for certain benefits because of birth defects associated with the mother's service in Vietnam that resulted in a permanent physical or mental disability.

The covered birth defects do not include conditions due to family disorders, birth-related injuries, or fetal or neonatal infirmities with well-established causes. A monetary allowance is paid at one of four disability levels based on the child's degree of permanent disability.

2013 VA Benefits for Children of Women Vietnam Veterans Born with Certain Birth Defects

	Level I	Level II	Level III	Level IV
Monthly Rate	$139	$303	$1,038	$1,769

Vocational Training: VA provides vocational training, rehabilitation services, and employment assistance to help these children prepare for and attain suitable employment. To qualify, an applicant must be a child receiving a VA monthly allowance for spina bifida or another covered birth defect and for whom VA has determined that achievement of a vocational goal is reasonably feasible. A child may not begin vocational training before his/her 18th birthday or the date he/she completes secondary schooling, whichever comes first. Depending on need and eligibility, a child may be provided up to 24 months of full-time training with the possibility of an extension of up to 24 months if it is needed to achieve the identified employment goal.

Other Benefits for Survivors

VA Home Loan Guaranty

A VA loan guaranty to acquire a home may be available to an unmarried spouse of a Veteran or Servicemember who died as a result of service-connected disabilities, a surviving spouse who remarries after age 57, or to a spouse of a Servicemember officially listed as MIA or who is currently a POW for more than 90 days. Spouses of those listed MIA/POW are limited to one loan. Surviving spouses of certain totally disabled Veterans whose disability may not have been the cause of death, may also be eligible for the VA loan guaranty.

"No-Fee" Passports

"No-fee" passports are available to immediate family members (spouse, children, parents, brothers and sisters) for the expressed purpose of visiting their loved one's grave or memorialization site at an American military cemetery on foreign soil. For additional information, write to the American Battle Monuments Commission, Courthouse Plaza II, Suite 500, 2300 Clarendon Blvd., Arlington, VA 22201, or telephone 703-696-6897, or visit www.abmc.gov

Burial and Memorial Benefits for Survivors

The Department of Veterans Affairs offers several burial and memorial benefits for eligible survivors and dependents. These benefits may include internment at a state or national Veterans cemetery, plot, marker and more. To learn more about these and other benefits please refer to Chapter 7 of this guide.

Chapter 14
Appeals of VA Claims Decisions

Veterans and other claimants for VA benefits have the right to appeal decisions made by a VA regional office, medical center or National Cemetery Administration (NCA) office. Typical issues appealed are disability compensation, pension, education benefits, recovery of overpayments, reimbursement for unauthorized medical services, and denial of burial and memorial benefits.

A claimant has one year from the date of the notification of a VA decision to file an appeal. The first step in the appeal process is for a claimant to file a written notice of disagreement with the VA regional office, medical center or national cemetery office that made the decision.

Following receipt of the written notice, VA will furnish the claimant a "Statement of the Case" describing what facts, laws, and regulations were used in deciding the case. To complete the request for appeal, the claimant must file a "Substantive Appeal" within 60 days of the mailing of the Statement of the Case, or within one year from the date VA mailed its decision, whichever period ends later.

Board of Veterans' Appeals
The Board of Veterans' Appeals ("the Board") makes decisions on appeals on behalf of the Secretary of Veterans Affairs. Although it is not required, a veterans service organization, an agent, or an attorney may represent a claimant. Appellants may present their cases in person to a member of the Board at a hearing in Washington, D.C., at a VA regional office or by videoconference.

Decisions made by the Board can be found at www.index.va.gov/search/va/bva.html. The pamphlet, "Understanding the Appeal Process," is available on the website or may be requested by writing: Mail Process Section (014), Board of Veterans' Appeals, 810 Vermont Avenue, NW, Washington, DC 20420.

U.S. Court of Appeals for Veterans Claims

A final Board of Veterans' Appeals decision that does not grant a claimant the benefits desired may be appealed to the U.S. Court of Appeals for Veterans Claims. The court is an independentbody, not part of the Department of Veterans Affairs.

Notice of an appeal must be received by the court with a postmark that is within 120 days after the Board of Veterans' Appeals mailed its decision. The court reviews the record considered by the Board of Veterans' Appeals. It does not hold trials or receive new evidence.

Appellants may represent themselves before the court or have lawyers or approved agents as representatives. Oral argument is held only at the direction of the court. Either party may appeal a decision of the court to the U.S. Court of Appeals for the Federal Circuit and may seek review in the Supreme Court of the United States.

Published decisions, case status information, rules and procedures, and other special announcements can be found at http://www.uscourts.cavc.gov/. The court's decisions can also be found in West's Veterans Appeals Reporter, and on the Westlaw and LEXIS online services. For questions, write the Clerk of the Court, 625 Indiana Ave. NW, Suite 900, Washington, DC 20004, or call (202) 501-5970.

Chapter 15
Military Medals and Records

Replacing Military Medals

Medals awarded while in active service are issued by the individual military services if requested by Veterans or their next of kin. Requests for replacement medals, decorations, and awards should be directed to the branch of the military in which the Veteran served. However, for Air Force (including Army Air Corps) and Army Veterans, the National Personnel Records Center (NPRC) verifies awards and forwards requests and verification to appropriate services.

Requests for replacement medals should be submitted on Standard Form 180, "Request Pertaining To Military Records," which may be obtained at VA offices or the Internet at www.va.gov/vaforms/. Forms, addresses, and other information on requesting medals can be found on the Military Personnel Records section of NPRC's Website at www.archives.gov/st-louis/military-personnel/index.html. For questions, call Military Personnel Records at (314) 801-0800 or e-mail questions to: MPR.center@nara.gov.

When requesting medals, type or clearly print the Veteran's full name, include the Veteran's branch of service, service number or Social Security number and provide the Veteran's exact or approximate dates of military service. The request must contain the signature of the Veteran or next of kin if the Veteran is deceased. If available, include a copy of the discharge or separation document, WDAGO Form 53-55 or DD Form 214.

If discharge or separation documents are lost, Veterans or the next of kin of deceased Veterans may obtain duplicate copies through the eBenefits portal (www.ebenefits.va.gov) or by completing forms found on the Internet at www.archives.gov/research/index.html and mailing or faxing them to the NPRC.

Alternatively, write the National Personnel Records Center, Military

Personnel Records, One Archives Drive, St. Louis, MO 63138-1002. Specify that a duplicate separation document is needed. The Veteran's full name should be printed or typed so that it can be read clearly, but the request must also contain the signature of the Veteran or the signature of the next of kin, if the Veteran is deceased. Include the Veteran's branch of service, service number or Social Security number and exact or approximate dates and years of service. Use Standard Form 180, "Request Pertaining To Military Records."

It is not necessary to request a duplicate copy of a Veteran's discharge or separation papers solely for the purpose of filing a claim for VA benefits. If complete information about the Veteran's service is furnished on the application, VA will obtain verification of service.

Correcting Military Records

The Secretary of a military department, acting through a Board for Correction of Military Records, has authority to change any military record when necessary to correct an error or remove an injustice. A correction board may consider applications for correction of a military record, including a review of a discharge issued by court-martial.

The Veteran, survivor, or legal representative must file a request for correction within three years of discovering an alleged error or injustice. The board may excuse failure to file within this time, however, if it finds it would be in the interest of justice. It is an applicant's responsibility to show why the filing of the application was delayed and why it would be in the interest of justice for the board to consider it despite the delay.

To justify a correction, it is necessary to show to the satisfaction of the board that the alleged entry or omission in the records was in error or unjust. Applications should include all available evidence, such as signed statements of witnesses or a brief of arguments supporting the correction. Application is made with DD Form 149, available at VA offices, Veterans organizations or visit www.dtic.mil/whs/directives/infomgt/forms/formsprogram.htm.

Review of Discharge from Military Service

Each of the military services maintains a discharge review board with authority to change, correct or modify discharges or dismissals not issued by a sentence of a general court-martial. The board has no authority to address medical discharges.

The Veteran or, if the Veteran is deceased or incompetent, the surviving spouse, next of kin or legal representative, may apply for a review of discharge by writing to the military department concerned, using DD Form 293 – "Application for the Review of Discharge from the Armed Forces of the United States." This form may be obtained at a VA regional office, from Veterans organizations or online at www. dtic.mil/whs/directives/infomgt/forms/formsprogram.htm.

However, if the discharge was more than 15 years ago, a Veteran must petition the appropriate Service's Board for Correction of Military Records using DD Form 149 – "Application for Correction of Military Records Under the Provisions of Title 10, U.S. Code, Section 1552." A discharge review is conducted by a review of an applicant's record and, if requested, by a hearing before the board.

Discharges awarded as a result of a continuous period of unauthorized absence in excess of 180 days make persons ineligible for VA benefits regardless of action taken by discharge review boards, unless VA determines there were compelling circumstances for the absence. Boards for the Correction of Military Records also may consider such cases.

Veterans with disabilities incurred or aggravated during active duty may qualify for medical or related benefits regardless of separation and characterization of service. Veterans separated administratively under other than honorable conditions may request that their discharge be reviewed for possible recharacterization, provided they file their appeal within 15 years of the date of separation.

Questions regarding the review of a discharge should be addressed to the appropriate discharge review board at the address listed on DD Form 293.

Physical Disability Board of Review

Veterans separated due to disability from Sept. 11, 2001, through Dec. 31, 2009, with a combined rating of 20 percent or less, as determined by the respective branch of service Physical Evaluation Board (PEB), and not found eligible for retirement, may be eligible for a review by the Physical Disability Board of Review (PDBR).

The PDBR was established to reassess the accuracy and fairness of certain PEB decisions, and where appropriate, recommend the correction of discrepancies and errors. A PDBR review will not lower the disability rating previously assigned by the PEB, and any correction may be made retroactively to the day of the original disability separation. As a result of the request for review by the PDBR, no further relief from the Board of Corrections of Military Records may be sought, and the recommendations by the PDBR, once accepted by the respective branch of service, is final. A comparison of these two boards, along with other PDBR information, can be viewed at www.health.mil/pdbr.

The Veteran or, if the Veteran is deceased or incompetent, the spouse or surviving spouse, next of kin or legal representative, may apply for a review using DD Form 294, "Application for a Review by the Physical Disability Board of Review (PDBR) of the Rating Awarded Accompanying a Medical Separation from the Armed Forces of the United States." As part of the review process, the PDBR considers the rating(s) previously awarded by VA. The completion of VA Form 3288, "Request for and Consent to Release of Information from Individual's Records," along with DD Form 294, allows the PDBR to request VA records. Both forms can be downloaded from the PDBR website at www.health.mil/pdbr. These forms may also be obtained at a VA Regional Office (VARO), from a veterans service organization (VSO) or online at www.dtic.mil/whs/directives/infomgt/forms/formsprogram.htm.

Chapter 16
Benefits Provided by Other Federal Agencies

Internal Revenue Service

This year many workers will qualify for the Earned Income Credit (EIC) because their income declined or they became unemployed. Tax refunds through the EIC and Child Tax Credit can help low- and moderate-income families cover day-to-day expenses such as utilities, rent, and child care. To learn more, visit www.irs.gov or consult a tax preparer.

Special Tax Considerations for Veterans

Disabled veterans may be eligible to claim a federal tax refund based on: an increase in the veteran's percentage of disability from VA or the combat-disabled veteran applying for, and being granted, Combat-Related Special Compensation, after an award for Concurrent Retirement and Disability. To do so, the disabled veteran will need to file the amended return, Form 1040X, Amended U.S. Individual Income Tax Return, to correct a previously filed Form 1040, 1040A or 1040EZ. An amended return cannot be e-filed. It must be filed as a paper return. Disabled veterans should include all documents from VA and any information received from Defense Finance and Accounting Services explaining proper tax treatment for the current year.

If needed, veterans should seek assistance from a competent tax professional before filing amended returns based on a disability determination. Refund claims based on an incorrect interpretation of the tax law could subject the veteran to interest and/or penalty charges. Complete information and requirements can be found at http://www.irs.gov/Individuals/Military/Special-Tax-Considerations-for-Veterans.

USDA Provides Loans for Farms and Homes

The U.S. Department of Agriculture (USDA) provides loans and guarantees to buy, improve or operate farms. Loans and guarantees are generally available for housing in towns with a population up to 20,000. Applications from Veterans have preference. For further information, contact Farm Service Agency or Rural Development, USDA, 1400 Independence Ave., S.W., Washington, DC 20250, or apply at local Department of Agriculture offices, usually located in county seats.

HUD Veteran Resource Center (HUDVET)

Housing and Urban Development (HUD) sponsors the Veteran Resource Center (HUDVET), which works with national Veterans service organizations to serve as a general information center on all HUD-sponsored housing and community development programs and services. To contact HUDVET, call 1-800-998-9999, TDD 800-483-2209, or visit www.hud.gov/hudvet.

Veterans Receive Naturalization Preference

Honorable active-duty service in the U.S. armed forces during a designated period of hostility allows an individual to naturalize without being required to establish any periods of residence or physical presence in the United States. A Servicemember who was in the United States, certain territories, or aboard an American public vessel at the time of enlistment, re-enlistment, extension of enlistment or induction, may naturalize even if he or she is not a lawful permanent resident.

On July 3, 2002, the president issued Executive Order 13269 establishing a new period of hostility for naturalization purposes beginning Sept. 11, 2001, and continuing until a date designated by a future Executive Order. Qualifying members of the armed forces who have served at any time during a specified period of hostility may immediately apply for naturalization using the current application, Form N-400, "Application for Naturalization". Additional information about filing and requirement fees and designated periods of hostility are available on the U.S. Citizenship and Immigration Services Website at www.uscis.gov.

Individuals who served honorably in the U.S. armed forces, but were no longer serving on active duty status as of Sept. 11, 2001, may still be naturalized without having to comply with the residence and physical presence requirements for naturalization if they filed Form N-400 while still serving in the U.S. armed forces or within six months of termination of their active duty service.

An individual who files the application for naturalization after the six-month period following termination of active-duty service is not exempt from the residence and physical presence requirements, but can count any period of active-duty service towards the residence and physical presence requirements. Individuals seeking naturalization under this provision must establish that they are lawful permanent residents (such status not having been lost, rescinded or abandoned) and that they served honorably in the U.S. armed forces for at least one year.

If a Servicemember dies as a result of injury or disease incurred or aggravated by service during a time of combat, the Servicemember's survivor(s) can apply for the deceased Servicemember to receive posthumous citizenship at any time within two years of the Service-member's death. The issuance of a posthumous certificate of citizenship does not confer U.S. citizenship on surviving relatives. However, a non-U.S. citizen spouse or qualifying family member may file for certain immigration benefits and services based upon their relationship to a Servicemember who died during hostilities or a non-citizen Servicemember who died during hostilities and was later granted posthumous citizenship.

For additional information, USCIS has developed a web page,www.uscis.gov/military, that contains information and links to services specifically for the military and their families. Members of the U.S. military and their families stationed around the world can also call USCIS for help with immigration services and benefits using a dedicated, toll-free help line at 1-877-CIS-4MIL (1-877-247-4645).

Small Business Administration (SBA)

Historically, Veterans do very well as small business entrepreneurs. Veterans interested in entrepreneurship and small business ownership should look to the U.S. Small Business Administration's Office of Veterans Business Development (OVBD) for assistance. OVBD conducts comprehensive outreach to Veterans, service-disabled Veterans, and Reservists of the U.S. military. OVBD also provides assistance to Veteran- and Reservist-owned small businesses. SBA is the primary federal agency responsible for assisting Veterans who own or are considering starting their own small businesses.

Among the services provided by SBA are business-planning assistance, counseling, and training through community based Veterans Business Outreach Centers. For more information, go to www.sba.gov/aboutsba/sbaprograms/ovbd/OVBD_VBOP.html. More than 1,000 university-based Small Business Development Centers; nearly 400 SCORE chapters (www.score.org/Veteran.html) with 11,000 volunteer counselors, many of whom are Veterans; and 100 Women's Business Centers.

SBA also manages a range of special small business lending programs at thousands of locations, ranging from Micro Loans to the Military-community-targeted Patriot Express Pilot Loan, to venture capital and Surety Bond Guarantees (www.sba.gov/services/financialassistance/index.html). Veterans also participate in all SBA federal procurement programs, including a special 3 percent federal procurement goal specifically for service-connected disabled Veterans, and SBA supports Veterans and others participating in international trade.

A special Military Reservist Economic Injury Disaster Loan (www.sba.gov/reservists) is available for self-employed Reservists whose small businesses may be damaged through the absence of the owner or an essential employee as a result of Title 10 activation to Active Duty.

A Veterans Business Development Officer is stationed at every SBA District Office to act as a guide to Veterans, and SBA offers a full range of self-paced small business planning assistance at www.sba.gov/survey/checklist/index.cgi for Veterans, Reservists, discharging Servicemembers, and their families. Information about the full range of services can be found at http://www.sba.gov/about-offices-content/1/2985, or by calling 202-205-6773 or 1-800-U-ASK-SBA (1-800-827-5722).

Social Security Administration

Monthly retirement, disability and survivor benefits under Social Security are payable to Veterans and dependents if the Veteran has earned enough work credits under the program. Upon the Veteran's death, a one-time payment of $255 also may be made to the Veteran's spouse or child. In addition, a Veteran may qualify at age 65 for Medicare's hospital insurance and medical insurance. Medicare protection is available to people who have received Social Security disability benefits for 24 months, and to insured people and their dependents who need dialysis or kidney transplants, or who have amyotrophic lateral sclerosis (more commonly known as Lou Gehrig's disease).

Since 1957, military service earnings for active duty (including active duty for training) have counted toward Social Security and those earnings are already on Social Security records. Since 1988, inactive duty service in the Reserve Component (such as weekend drills) has also been covered by Social Security. Servicemembers and Veterans are credited with $300 credit in additional earnings for each calendar quarter in which they received active duty basic pay after 1956 and before 1978.

Veterans who served in the military from 1978 through 2001 are credited with an additional $100 in earnings for each $300 in active duty basic pay, up to a maximum of $1,200 a year. No additional Social Security taxes are withheld from pay for these extra credits. Veterans who enlisted after Sept. 7, 1980, and did not complete at least 24 months of active duty or their full tour of duty, may not be able to receive the additional earnings. Check with Social Security for details. Additional earnings will no longer be credited for military service periods after 2001.

Also, non-contributory Social Security earnings of $160 a month may be credited to Veterans who served after Sept. 15, 1940, and before 1957, including attendance at service academies. For information, call 1-800-772-1213 or visit www.socialsecurity.gov/. (Note: Social Security cannot add these extra earnings to the record until an application is filed for Social Security benefits).

Armed Forces Retirement Homes

Veterans are eligible to live in the Armed Forces Retirement Homes located in Gulfport, Miss., or Washington, D.C., if their active duty military service is at least 50 percent enlisted, warrant officer or limited duty officer if they qualify under one of the following categories:

1. Are 60 years of age or older; and were discharged or released under honorable conditions after 20 or more years of active service.
2. Are determined to be incapable of earning a livelihood

because of a service-connected disability incurred in the line of duty.
3. Served in a war theater during a time of war declared by Congress or were eligible for hostile-fire special pay and were discharged or released under honorable conditions; and are determined to be incapable of earning a livelihood because of injuries, disease or disability.
4. Served in a women's component of the armed forces before June 12, 1948; and are determined to be eligible for admission due to compelling personal circumstances.

Eligibility determinations are based on rules prescribed by the Home's Chief Operating Officer. Veterans are not eligible if they have been convicted of a felony or are not free from alcohol, drug or psychiatric problems. Married couples are welcome, but both must be eligible in their own right. At the time of admission, applicants must be capable of living independently.

The Armed Forces Retirement Home is an independent federal agency. For information, call 1-800-332-3527 or 1-800-422-9988, or visit www.afrh.gov/.

Commissary and Exchange Privileges

Unlimited commissary and exchange store privileges in the United States are available to honorably discharged Veterans with a service-connected disability rated at 100 percent or totally disabling, and to the unremarried surviving spouses and dependents of Servicemembers who die on active duty, military retirees, recipients of the Medal of Honor, and Veterans whose service-connected disability was rated 100 percent or totally disabling at the time of death. Certification of total disability is done by VA. National Guard Reservists and their dependents may also be eligible. Privileges overseas are governed by international law and are available only if agreed upon by the foreign government concerned

Though these benefits are provided by DOD, VA does provide assistance in completing DD Form 1172, "Application for Uniformed Services Identification and Privilege Card." For detailed information, contact the nearest military installation.

U.S. Department of Health and Human Services

The U.S. Department of Health and Human Services provides funding to states to help low-income households with their heating and home energy costs under the Low Income Home Energy Assistance Program (LIHEAP). LIHEAP can also assist with insulating homes to make them more energy efficient and reduce energy costs. The LIHEAP program in your community determines if your household's income qualifies for the program. To find out where to apply call 1-866-674-6327 or e-mail energy@ncat.org 7 a.m.- 5 p.m. (Mountain Time). More information can be found at www.acf.hhs.gov/programs/ocs/liheap/#index.html

Notes

Notes